real saved folks

Sonnie Beverly

Real Saved Folks
by Sonnie Beverly

ISBN 1-58169-036-3
For Worldwide Distribution
Printed in the U.S.A.

Third Story Window
An Imprint of Genesis Communications, Inc.
P.O. Box 91011 • Mobile, AL 36691
800-367-8203
Email: GenesisCom@aol.com

TABLE OF CONTENTS

ACKNOWLEDGEMENTS

My children, Shaun, Shannon and Shannell, who are as much a part of me as my eyes or my arms, or my hands or my nose, I acknowledge that you are God's most precious gifts to me. You have brought me only much pride, joy and peace in knowing that you know the Father like I know the Father; therefore, you will forever be abundantly blessed in every area in your lives. This is my desire for you. I cannot imagine my life without each one of you. My inspiration, my comfort, my husband Andrá: I thank God for the blessing you are and thanks, partner, for opening my eyes to that which I could not see.

It seems that the special people in my life come in twos. I would like to thank my Board, my mother, Claudette Beverly and My Aunt Gwen, Gwendolyn Mitchell, my two anchors who keep me grounded no matter what, giving me both sides of the story, making sure I see all of everything for what it is and for what it could potentially become to ensure I make the best possible decisions about my life. My other two play mothers, Jean Hockaday and Katie White, you have always been that and so much more to me. My cousins, Cal and Claudia, you twins marked my twins. I thought you were supposed to skip a generation. My two absolute best friends who have been with me through it all: LaFarn and Terry. My two sisters in Christ who know how to get their praise and prayer on, who have been my source of inspiration since coming to this new land: Harriette and P.A. To each and every one of the Chappells. Thank you for opening your arms ever so wide and making us a part of you. I will always love you.

Thanks to the individuals who read my manuscript in its roughest form and encouraged me to pursue it because the masses needed it; my original publisher, Elder Gwendolyn Young; my 5:00 a.m. prayer partner Patrice; my original editor Charlene Fain of Writeous Communications; my other editor and play twin, Karen; my cousin, Keith; avid reader Sheila; my brother C.B.; my play brother, Jene and his sister, my college roommate Vanessa; my other college roommate, D.C. Pam; and my brothers in Christ, Leroy Mincey and Benton Aladin of DAB Media.

And I just have to mention two of the most wonderful women I have ever met in my entire life. Dorcas Henegan and Barbara Welch, your professionalism, intelligence, maturity, warmth and kindness completely overwhelmed me when I reentered corporate America. Vickye, you are a true sweetheart. And Russell, thank you for always being my friend. My play cousin, Octavia Lee Hall, let's do it. My real, true, flesh and blood cousins, Kim and Kitten. It ain't over until God says it's over, so let's totally surrender and let Him do His thing.

INTRODUCTION

Women just seem to automatically rise up and do what needs to be done for their home and their families. Single mothers are super women who have to serve as both mother and father, and some married women have to do the same if there is a non-participating father in the home. These super women have to work one or more jobs outside the home, pay the bills, and fix what's broken or hurt—whether it be a toy or a child's or a man's feelings. They have to shop, cook, clean, chauffeur, help with homework, go to the doctor, attend school functions, discipline, train, go to church, spend private time with God, find time for self, exercise, and get their families through tragedies as well as emergencies. They go to the movies, socialize with family and friends, deal with jealousy, envy, and misunderstanding, and still look good. Wonder Woman can't touch today's Super Woman.

To say balancing all of the responsibilities of today's Super Woman is a struggle would be an understatement. Yet women are doing it every day—some better than others. The balancing formula can be improved upon as long as the main ingredient is included—faith in the Word of God.

Real Saved Folks is about Nicole Riley, a real super woman, born-again Christian, totally sold out for Jesus, who discovers that she is just a real woman with the same needs and desires as most women. She gives up everything to escape the bondage of religious tradition, the pain of family tragedy, and certain spiritual death to seek God's best for her and her children's lives. Armed with little more than total faith and confidence in the Word of God, she stands on Genesis 3:12 and, like Abraham, leaves her land of familiarity to move to a new city and join a new church family where she believes she will have joy, peace, and satisfaction. Niki soon finds out that the tests, trials, tribulations, and temptations of the world are just as prevalent inside the church as they are on the outside. She meets and befriends two Christian sisters who become her greatest challenge when she stumbles across true love. Her two best friends are the only things that stand between her and the man God created just for her. Through disappointment, family tragedy, the stress of uprooting and moving, single parenting, job frustrations, trying to fit in, friendship, love relationships, depression and denial, faith combined with love conquers all as the real saved folks, often humorously, believe God through their real struggles and in the end find out that they were really and truly saved by God's grace.

DEDICATION

I do not believe in coincidences, so the fact that the day I am writing this dedication is the one year anniversary of when my daddy went home to be with the Lord is symbolic of the fact that I feel very strongly about dedicating this book to him—Mr. James Booker-T Harris—my hero, my earthly provider, my rock, my strength, my courage, my confidence, my savior from Mom's wrath, my inspiration, my safety net, always there for any and everything my whole entire life. Only by the grace of God have I made it through this year without your physical presence in my life.

I also dedicate this book to Cherry, Tiger, and Angel, my family that went way too soon, the wrong way, for all the wrong reasons. We had a ball when we were together before and we will have a ball when we are together again.

I love you all very, very much.

For the Lord himself shall descend from heaven with a shout,
with the voice of the archangel, and with the trump of God:
and the dead in Christ shall rise first:
Then we which are alive and remain shall be caught up together
with them in the clouds, to meet the Lord in the air:
and so shall we ever be with the Lord.

1 Thessalonians 4:16-17

CHAPTER 1

"Go get us another hit," Rae told Brenda.

"Gimme some money," Brenda said.

"I ain't got no mo' money. Where's your money?" asked Rae.

"Gone," said Brenda.

"Gone? You mean all the money's gone already? I ain't even bought no food yet. What I'ma do now?"

Rae paused to think. "What am I doing in here? I got to get outta here. What I'ma do?" Turning and looking at her "git-high" buddy, she asked, "How you gonna feed your kids, Brenda?"

"Steal some food," was Brenda's response.

"Girl, you know them cameras pick up everything nowadays. They can pick up the writing on the labels of the food you just put in your pocket," Rae reminded her.

She paused again, deep in thought, confused about something in particular. *How could this have happened? I listened to my cousin, Niki, all the time. I believed what she said. Why did I do what I just did?*

"Well, is Jesus going to feed my kids, Rae?" asked Brenda, tapping her nails on the table.

Snapping to attention, face all wrinkled up from the revelation that just hit her, Rae said, "That just blows my high, 'cause if He don't, I gotta take something for me and my kids to eat and pray I don't get busted. Let's get outta here."

They stepped over bodies sprawled all over the floor and avoided looking at the addicts sitting in the corners trying in vain to find that first rush again, as they left the house. Rae shook her head disappointed, frustrated, and downright angry that they had nothing to show for their money. Not even a very good high.

Around the corner from the crack house Rae spotted a pay phone. "Wait a minute, Brenda, I got to make a call 'cause I don't understand this mess. Hold up," she said, disgusted with someone else besides herself, but not sure who. She picked up the receiver and made a local collect call.

RIIIINNGG!! Niki snatched up the receiver at the same time looking at the clock that read 3:30 a.m.

1

"HELLO?" she said very alert in spite of the fact that she was awakened from a sound sleep. Even though she answered the phone in her normal way, the person on the other end heard "What's wrong?" in her voice. Niki had been sleeping very light lately, jumping every time the phone rang, and hoping not to hear that somebody else had been killed. She was especially jumpy when the phone rang at this time of morning.

"Collect call from Rae. Will you accept the charges?" asked the voice.

"Yes," Niki quickly replied.

"Go ahead, ma'am," instructed the voice.

"Nik, Jesus done let us down. I thought you said He would never let us down."

Niki, wide awake now, felt relief that apparently no one was dead. "Rae, what are you talking about?"

"Me and my friend, right, we got our checks today, right? And we cashed 'em, see, and now we ain't got no money, and our kids don't got nothing to eat, so you know I'ma hafta steal 'em somethin' to eat, right? So what me and my friend want to know is why Jesus let us spend all our money on crack? I mean I told her all that good stuff you be telling me. Now she ain't goin' to believe me no more. So why Jesus let us do that Nik, huh? Why?"

"Jesus *let* y'all?" Niki responded sitting up in the bed, realizing the tragedy that led to her cousin's question and attempting to provoke her to think about what she was asking.

"Well, the devil made us, but yeah, Jesus let us. I mean, why He ain't stop us?" Rae asked, seriously expecting a logical answer.

Niki rubbed her eyes as if that would help to clear her mind. "Let me get this straight. The devil *made* y'all and Jesus *let* y'all. Did y'all have any say so in the matter?" asked Niki.

"Nope," Rae answered quickly. Then before Niki could jump all over her for not taking responsibility for her own actions, she continued, "Well, yeah, but you the one who told me Jesus would never leave me or forsake me." She needed one last shot at dodging responsibility. "And you the one that explained to me about salvation so I could believe God sent Jesus to die for my sins."

Now that she realized that she was totally responsible for her own actions and that her cousin knew it, too, and there was no one else to blame but herself, Rae wanted to drop that part of the conversation and get to that good part that always made her feel better after she had messed up.

"I do believe that He came down to earth from heaven and walked the earth as a man. And when His time was up He let them hang Him on the cross where He died so He could go to hell for me and take back all the devil's power that Adam gave up when he ate the apple with his stupid self. Now we don't have to get beat up by the devil. Right?" asked Rae, her intellectual spirit rising up and taking control over the crack spirit that had led her astray.

2

"You got it," Niki said, relieved and feeling very good about the fact that her constant preaching had not fallen on deaf ears. "Go on."

"So when Jesus died on the cross, He did what He came to do for us that took three days. Then God raised Him from the dead," said Rae.

"Yep. What else?" coached Niki.

"I believe that really happened, Nik. And I asked Jesus to come into my life and be my Lord and Savior. I accepted God's gift of salvation, and I believe that I'm saved 'cause I accepted the gift," Rae testified. She was excited now, pumping herself up, remembering the many hours of conversation she had had with her cousin on this subject and how it made her feel.

"You preaching now, Cous'; go on girl," Niki said, feeling a shout coming up, herself.

"I don't have to do anything to get saved 'cause God's grace saved me."

"Hallelujah!" praised Niki.

"Won't nothing I could do to get saved but believe what I just said, and I do Nik, I promise you I do," Rae confessed.

"So what's the problem, Cous'?" Niki asked.

"Well, if Jesus is my Lord and Savior, why He ain't save my money from the crack dealers?"

"Rae, why do you think I always say you got to get to where you can hear some Word?"

"So I can hear some word," Rae couldn't resist.

"Ha, ha, you trying to be funny, but you are exactly right. The only thing that has happened to you is that you are no longer going to hell when you die. You are saved from eternal damnation because you asked Jesus to come into your life like you just said. When He comes back for His people, if it's in our lifetime, you'll be among those taken up with the rest of us Christians. But while you are still on this earth, baby, there are some things you got to do. You need to get to where you can hear God's Word, His instructions on how to live in this world until you get up outta here," explained Niki.

"Yeah, I remember you said that BIBLE stands for Basic Instructions Before Leaving Earth."

"Well, since you be paying attention, tell me, how does faith come?"

"Not by hearing the Word one time, but by hearing and hearing and hearing and hearing and hearing and hearing and just keep on hearing the Word of God."

"That's it," Niki said, smiling like a proud teacher. "The more you hear, the easier it'll become to do what you gotta do."

"I can't be in church all the time like you, Cous'."

"Hey, well, then there are other means by which you can hear the Word. Listen to the tapes I gave you. As your faith grows by hearing the Word of God, you'll want more."

3

"For real?" asked Rae, wanting to be into it like her cousin.

"Yeah, and not only that, but the Word will make you strong enough to turn your back on those people and things you don't want in your life. When they come around you, you will talk to them like I'm talking to you, and they will get saved."

"Cous', I could never talk like you."

"Believe me, when the Word gets in you, it just comes out," said Niki. "But you got to be stronger in *your thing* than they are in *their thing,* 'cause the strongest will win over the other. So if they are stronger in drugs than you are in the Word of God, then they will suck you back in, which is what has happened."

"That is sho' nuff what happened," said Rae.

"Now you got to get strong in the Word of God before you can be around them. But don't fool yourself. It's work like anything else worthwhile. You are responsible for taking the time and putting forth the effort to make yourself strong in the Word. But you *can* do it cause the greater One lives on the inside of you," said Niki.

"I heard that," said Rae.

"But Rae…" said Niki.

"Huh?" answered Rae.

Niki wanted to make sure Rae understood the course of events that led up to this point. "He ain't going to *make you* do nothing. He ain't even going to *stop you* from doing what you want to do. It's always *your choice.* Remember your choices? Life or death, blessings or cursings. He told you what to do when He said, 'Choose life.' Just gave you the answer, and we still don't get it right sometimes. Some of us choose death even after He told us point blank and period to choose life," Niki said.

"Yeah, you right," Rae said, all trace of a previous high completely gone.

"He's right there for you when you choose to do the right thing. He'll help you, but you gotta do the work, baby. You got lots of people rooting and praying for you that you don't even know about. So you can't lose with Jesus. He will help you do what you decide to do as long as it lines up with the Word," said Niki.

"Yeah, that's that good talk I like to hear. I'm going to church Sunday so I can hear some Word. I'm going to find somebody preaching the Word on TV. And I'm going to read my Bible," Rae said excitedly. Then suddenly solemn, "Cous'?"

"Yeah, baby?" responded Niki.

"You think God forgives me?"

"Did you ask Him to?"

"God, please forgive me," pleaded Rae.

"He just did, Cous'. Go get some rest and pray in tongues until you fall asleep."

"Okay. Are you really moving to Zion?" asked Rae.

"Got to," said Niki.

"I'm gonna miss you, Cous'. Who will I call now?"

"Call Jesus, baby, He's already there," said Niki.

"I believe that. I love you, Cous'," said Rae.

"I love you, too, baby. You know what to do; now just do it."

"Okay."

"Promise?"

"I promise."

"Okay, then. I'll bring some groceries, so don't go stealing nothing," warned Niki.

"Bless you, Cous'," said Rae.

"Bye, bye."

"Thanks, Nik."

"Thank God, baby."

CHAPTER 2

They were finally all set to go after trying to leave for over an hour.

"Where is Mia and Maya? Taj, go get your sisters. No, I'll get them," Niki said, trying desperately to round up the children so they could get on the road to Zion. She had had it up to here with Fulton and was ready to start totally over. She didn't know if she would get divorced or believe God to restore her marriage. She was in a state of limbo. All she knew right now was that she had to leave; there was no way that she could stay in Fulton. The walls were closing in on her; and with her claustrophobia, she felt herself losing her grip on the situation. She had to do something before that happened.

When she went into the house, she found Mia and Maya, both on their granddaddy's lap on the sofa, clinging, hugging, crying, and slobbering all over him. He didn't mind at all. His heart was breaking. What would he do now that he wouldn't have his "reasons for living" to cater to every day?

Jim was the definition of grandparent, a child's natural ally. If his grandchildren wanted something, he bought it. Niki would insist that they earn some of the gifts, which always started an argument between her and her dad.

"They are just kids, they don't have to work for nothing. We are supposed to give them things to make them happy. Besides, I'm grateful for two things: that I can afford to buy them things and that I'm around to see them enjoy the things I can buy them. So let me enjoy myself with my grandchildren, please, thank you," Jim would say.

Niki's relationship with her dad had become a little strained since she had given him grandchildren because Jim usurped her strict discipline every chance he got. Sam, Niki's husband, was a silent partner and just allowed Niki to do whatever she deemed best in all situations. Sam was otherwise occupied with his so-called recreational drug use that had been taking up more and more of his productive time and money. He did all he could to keep Niki off his case. He wasn't about to give her a reason to come down on him, which she did so well. So when he had an opportunity to get in her good graces by taking her side against anybody, he did so; quietly though, because he didn't want to ruffle any other feathers either. "Maintain the peace" was Sam's motto.

"I don't want to go!" screamed Mia.

"I love you, Granddaddy," sobbed Maya, holding on to his neck for dear life.

Niki, realizing it would take extremely gentle coercion to get the girls away from their granddaddy and into the car and still avoid a dramatic fallout, said calmly and lovingly, "Come on, girls, we have to go. Granddaddy will be down to visit us maybe next week, knowing him. He'll probably be there in time enough to help us unpack. Come on, now."

There was no move toward their letting go; Granddaddy was holding on just as tight as the girls. Niki decided that she would have to physically pry the girls away from their granddaddy, whom they adored. Mia fell on the floor as Niki pulled her up and dragged her by one arm out the door. Jim, wiping tears from his eyes, followed them out the door, assisting Maya who was reluctantly dragging her feet.

Outside by the car was Taj, Sam, Grandma, and Grandma's sister, Aunt Katie. The car was packed, gassed up, and ready to go. Taj, trying to be a man in a 12-year-old body, assisted Niki in putting the girls in the back seat. Niki made her final round of quick hugs and jumped in the driver's seat. After kissing everybody one last time, Taj got in the front passenger seat feeling torn apart and confused, trying hard to figure out what to do.

"Bye, love you, see ya, come to Zion, we'll call you when we get there," Niki said as she pulled off waving to all the teary eyes standing in the driveway.

Taj looked at Niki, who was smiling. She appeared to be trying to hold in an outburst of some kind. Then he looked at the girls in the back seat wailing like their world was coming to an end. They were hugging each other and blubbering all over the back seat. Taj felt what they felt. He didn't care that now he was the man. He wanted to cry, too. He was being taken away from the only home he had ever known, from the people he adored and who adored him. He hurt just as much as his sisters did. He was really going to miss his family—they had spoiled him rotten. Who would do that now? Surely not his mother. She was too into "Train up a child in the way he should go, and when he is old he will not depart from it." He remembered her telling Grandma, "Pastor said that train means to *make them*." From that point on, if they didn't do what she said right away, she didn't hesitate to *make them*. They quickly learned to do what she said the first time. Granddaddy thought this was cruel and unusual punishment. "You don't even give them a chance, Niki. You are supposed to tell them at least twice," he would argue on his grandchildren's behalf when they were disciplined for not responding immediately to their mother's commands.

Reality began to set in that Taj would have no allies to rescue him when his mother got on her soapbox. He began to feel terrified. He wanted to scream, "HELP!! Save me Granddaddy; let me stay and live with you." When he looked over at his mother, he was even further confused. He had wanted to cry, but when he saw the big silly grin she had on her face, he couldn't help but laugh himself. "Oh well," Taj thought, "her mind's made up, so we can forget about changing it."

Driving down the interstate, Niki felt liberated for the first time in her life. She was going to do it God's way. She had had a lot of conversation with God over the last year. A year ago when she clearly heard in her spirit that it was okay for her to leave town, she had followed every leading, every prompting, every urging she received from the Holy Spirit immediately, because this was a life or death situation. She could not afford to mess up. She had lost one whole household full of family. *Doggone if I'm going to lose anything else,* she thought. She was committed to distancing herself from anything that posed a threat to her well-being or that of her children. She was going to eliminate any form of sin from her life and work totally for the Lord.

When Niki got "for real" saved six years ago, she was convinced that when she had been baptized years earlier at age nine she had loved the Lord Jesus Christ with all her heart; He was constantly on her mind. However, she still always did everything she could get away with, right or wrong. Because she didn't realize a lot of it was wrong, she didn't have a problem doing it. After she heard the true Word of God, she began to question her salvation since her conscience had not bothered her when she had committed sins. The Word told her that she should at least feel bad even if she had trouble not sinning right away since it takes time to break some habits.

She wanted to know for sure if she was saved or not, so she called a preacher friend of hers.

"Rev, I know I believed all about Jesus at nine years old when I got baptized even though I didn't know and wasn't taught how to live according to the Word of God. But during all that time, I loved Jesus and accepted Him as my Lord and Savior. However, I'm not sure if I'm saved because the Bible says without holiness no man shall see the Lord. God knows I ain't been living holy—even a little bit. So now I don't know what happened to me when I got baptized at nine. Am I saved, Rev?"

Rev, having both the smarts of how to deal with people and the spiritual knowledge of what they need, would lead, guide, and direct you into truth without ever coming right out and telling you what to do. Rev said, "Niki, since you have some doubt, why don't you do whatever you need to do to remove all doubt about your salvation?"

"Like what, Rev?" asked Niki.

"What would give you an assurance that you will spend eternity with Jesus, knowing what you know now?" he asked.

"Starting all over and doing it the right way," she answered.

"Then go for it," Rev encouraged.

She thought about it. Then the revelation hit her. "Oh, I get it," she shouted. "Thanks, Rev. I know what to do. Are you coming to my baptism?"

When Niki went down in the water that second time, she felt the change. Had she gone down or not, felt anything or not, her faith in what she believed Jesus did for her 2,000 years ago on the cross was enough to get her into heaven, and that she knew for sure. She just wanted to do something to show God, to pay Jesus back, to show that she was not ashamed, but very proud to be a child of God. So she invited everybody she knew to come to her baptism.

"Haven't you already been baptized one time?" asked her friends.

"Yeah, but even though I was born into the kingdom of God when I made the choice at nine years old, I didn't act like it. I'm doing it again because I want to start over and *act* like I've been born into the kingdom of God this time. I got to do it God's way," Niki would explain.

"Oh, okay, yeah, huh, uh. Gone, then girl," her friends would say looking at her like she was on some illegal substance.

"No, for real. I wallowed in mess and didn't have to. Now I'm learning how to step around it. I don't have to do that wild and crazy stuff I used to do. I want to forget all that old stuff and just live to please God and show Jesus how much I appreciate what He did for me."

"All right, Niki, you don't have to preach a sermon."

Now Niki, the extremist, went to zero tolerance for sin. This zero tolerance level caused major problems. It all but destroyed her marriage, especially with the challenges Sam was already having. Since nobody around her changed, she—being a new born-again Christian—tried to singlehandedly save the world and nearly drove herself and everybody around her crazy. She needed balance. She needed to get around people who understood her, who lived like she wanted to live—totally for Christ.

CHAPTER 3

The girls eventually stopped crying and fell asleep during the long car ride. They were pretty much quiet the whole ride to Zion. Taj drifted in and out of consciousness, feeling a need to keep his mom company, although she seemed perfectly content and preoccupied with something. They made a couple of restroom and fuel stops, buying snacks and fast food.

Finally they arrived in their new home town, their new apartment, their new world. The movers were scheduled to arrive at 10 a.m. the next morning, so tonight they would have to use the sleeping bags on the plush carpet. On her earlier trip to Zion to finalize the lease contract on the apartment, Niki had gone shopping for a few things to hold them until the movers arrived with all of their stuff.

The apartment was bigger and more beautiful than Niki expected it to be. After living in a house for such a long time, even having gotten rid of a lot of their possessions through yard sales, gifts to others, and regular visits to the Salvation Army truck, they still had a lot of stuff. Niki was a true pack rat, always able to justify the need to keep something. As she surveyed the apartment, she felt that it should be big enough to hold the things she couldn't bring herself to part with. *We'll see when the movers get here*, she thought

At about 9:00 p.m., there was a knock on the door. Looking through the peephole into the lighted hallway, Niki recognized one of the movers.

"Hey, Tony. What are you doing here so early?"

"Ms. Riley, we had to move everything up on the schedule. So we took a chance and left early with your load so that we could get back for this big job scheduled to start in the morning. We just came on down. If we can't do it, well heck, we'll stay overnight and move your things in the morning like we planned to do in the first place," explained Tony.

Considering that it took about three hours to get the stuff on the truck, Niki figured it would be around midnight when they would be finished moving everything in. On a weeknight, Niki didn't want to disturb her new neighbors. However, to get this over as soon as possible was not a bad idea. Her neighbors would just have to understand.

"No, that's fine. The sooner, the better. Bring it on," instructed Niki, excited that her new life was about to be underway.

10

"Yes, ma'am," said Tony, relieved. He went downstairs to inform Mike that the move was on.

"Let's get this done!" he said to Mike.

Back in the apartment, Niki was clearing the path for the movers. "Kids, get out of the way, the movers are here."

"Yeah, our TV is here," said Maya.

"My PlayStation, thank you, Lord!" shouted Taj.

Tony and Mike were not big guys, but either they were especially strong, or they just knew how to lift furniture so that it appeared that they were strong. Niki had observed Mike, the smallest of the two, lift a big, heavy dresser on his back by himself and was very impressed. Niki owned a lot of mirrors and glass. She was concerned about breakage and always included in her prayer, "Lord, let there be no damage to my stuff."

T&M Movers were recommended to Niki by a reliable source who assured her that they were very professional businessmen and very conscientious with their customer's goods. That and the fact that they were half the price of the big name national movers made Niki decide to give the brothers some business.

Unloading the truck did take about three hours. It probably should have taken a little more time, especially with the increased level of difficulty of going up a flight of stairs, but these guys were on a mission and sped things up a bit wherever possible. They got the job done in record time, but it didn't help Niki's stress level one bit. Thank God she didn't have a refrigerator to move.

Two and a half hours into the job, fatigue was beginning to set in on Tony and Mike. Their patience was wearing thin with each other, and they were beginning to have minor arguments.

"Why didn't you grab the table, man?" a perturbed Tony asked Mike.

"Tony, man, I thought you had it. Why didn't *you* just grab the little table?" responded an annoyed Mike, feeling that Tony wanted him to do more than his fair share of the work.

"You always saving somethin' for somebody else to do. You need to come off that junk, Mike man," Tony warned.

"Man, shut up, man. It was right there. All you had to do was stack the table on your other stuff and take it on in," said Mike.

"Forget it, man; I got the table, just shut up," Tony said clearly frustrated.

Niki, witnessing the altercation and praying that they didn't get too loud with it, figured that they may have been too tired to make the long drive back to Virginia.

"Why don't you guys get some rest before you head back?" she suggested.

"Look, we don't have it like that. We have to *be there* in the morning, not *be on our way* there. So just let us finish up so we can get on our way," snapped Tony, all of his courteous professionalism tapped out.

"Excuse me," mumbled Niki and made herself scarce.

She had done her part directing where to put the furniture. All the major stuff was in place to her satisfaction. She had told them that the rest of the stuff left to be brought in could just be put wherever there was empty space on the floor. She and the kids could deal with it once it was in the apartment, so she left them to finish up.

"Not so fast, man, I'm walking backwards up the steps," Tony yelled at Mike as they carried in a huge box together.

Niki heard their loud voices and heavy footsteps from all the way in her bedroom and prayed, "Lord, overtake them with Your peace, and please don't let them break anything. Refresh them with Your energy to finish this job and have a safe trip back, in Jesus' name."

Finally the last item was moved in, and Tony presented Niki with the bill for their work. In return, after doublechecking the amount, Niki handed him an envelope. After counting the cash, the men thanked her and beat a hasty retreat down the stairs to get back on the road.

Niki looked around at all the boxes, bags, suitcases, and other stuff. *Where do I start? I'll start by sleeping on it. After a good night's rest, I'll set a schedule to get this apartment in living condition and not stop until it's home sweet home,* she thought. The kids had jumped in their beds as soon as Tony and Mike had put them up. They'd been fast asleep for over an hour.

As Niki stretched out on her bed, she was overwhelmed with thanksgiving, excitement, and hopefulness for a bright future. She knew way deep down inside that whatever God had in store for her was so awesome that it was going to make everything she had been through to get here worth it.

CHAPTER 4

"Mommy, I'm hungry," Mia said directly into her mother's ear around 8:00 a.m.

"Huh? Huh? What? What time is it?" Niki asked, waking up, trying to get her bearings, adjusting to the unfamiliar room. For a second she thought, *Where am I?* Then, becoming increasingly awake, she realized that this was the first day of her new life. She jumped up, grabbed Mia and squeezed her until she squealed.

"Thank you, Lord, we made it! Praise You Jesus! Glory to God! Hallelujah! Praise You, Father! If I had ten thousand tongues I couldn't thank You enough, Father! Praise You, praise You, praise You, praise You, praise You!"

Niki went through the apartment maneuvering her way around the stuff that the movers had left, just as she'd instructed, anywhere there was an empty space.

The kids were used to their mother "getting her praise on." She said her victory was in her praise. They liked her when she was in "praise mode." Then they knew everything was all right—not like when she was quiet and deep in thought with that serious look on her face. They worried then. They worried when she was quiet and not smiling because it was her nature to smile and talk all the time, especially about God, Jesus, the Word of God and about what great things He had done for her.

Their mom was a WYSIWYG: What You See Is What You Get. She wore her feelings on her sleeve. When she was happy, everybody knew it; and when she was upset, everybody knew it. When she was going through something hard, everybody knew it; and when all was well, everybody knew it. Niki didn't much fear or care, for that matter, about what people thought or said about her. Her goal was to please God, not man. So she did exactly what she believed the Lord told her to do.

When she believed the Lord told her to leave her good paying job, she did, even though people thought she had lost her mind to leave a perfectly good job while still dealing with a husband on drugs. But had she not, her house would probably have been destroyed from within because of the drug use that was going on in there while she was at work. It could very well have become a glorified crack house had she not listened to God and moved on her faith by leaving her job to come home. She ended up saving her house and family from the ravages of drugs.

When Niki was able to be home full time, she came face to face with demons that were trying to destroy her family. And she went to war. She threw herself into the things of God, church, ministry, praying, volunteering, Bible study, and singing in the choir. When her family and friends saw her coming, they jokingly called her Rev. Riley or Sister Niki. As she grew in the things of God, the name calling was a compliment to her. It let her know that she was on the right track, living for Jesus; and everyone, especially those that called her those names, knew it.

She believed that she was pleasing God and that He would protect her and provide for her and her family and that nothing could by any means harm them. She lived by her faith because she learned that that is the only thing that pleases God. Her primary purpose for living became to please God, even if everyone else was displeased with her. She believed that if she strived to please God, then everything else she needed, wanted, or desired would be given to her. It had to. That is what the Word of God said, and if she didn't believe anything else, she believed everything that she read in the Bible.

After coming to the revelation that her husband had no desire to do what it took to please God or stop using drugs, she had a little talk with God.

"Father, I can control myself, and to a degree my children, but there is nothing else left for me to do about Sam. We've been through every drug rehab hospital, program, every kind of drug therapy, marriage and family counseling available, and he's still way over there and I'm way over here with You. I got to tell You, Lord, although I know You already know, but I just don't want it anymore. Of course I will do whatever You want me to do. If You say stay in this city, in this marriage, I will and believe You to make it right. But I want out of this marriage and this city. I have had it. I am ready to get on with my life and stop having to stand guard and protect my house and children from the drug users and pushers. I want to be able to trust everyone I live with. Tell me what to do, Lord."

Over the next few weeks, Niki got rid of everything in the house except what she was using. She emptied their attic, basement, and garage—any place she had stuff stored. Then she cleaned the house, every nook and cranny. Having acquired some nice items over the years, she worked with what she had to make the house look good enough to showcase in a magazine. It sparkled with all her glass and mirrors. She was quite pleased and wondered why she had never seen that level of beauty before.

As she was standing in the living room admiring how nice the house looked, the Lord spoke directly to her spirit. What she heard would change her life forever.

"Put the house on the market. You are moving to Zion," said a voice from deep within her spirit.

Her knees began to buckle. She had to sit down. That was one place she always wanted to live. She had been there once and loved it. She had been watching a TV ministry for the last few years which was based there. She had become a partner with the ministry and was truly blessed by the pastor. She could identify with the people in the congregation—they even looked like her. She could see herself being a member at the church.

Once she told a friend, "If I ever leave this city, I am going straight to Way Makers Ministries in Zion, 'cause that is my kind of church. The pastor always preaches exactly what I need to hear every time I tune in. I got to get to that church." She had heard nice things about the city, too; that it was a land of opportunity and all.

The next day she had met with a realtor, and two weeks later the house was sold. It was so God-orchestrated that Niki was fired up about what to do next. Surely she was about to enter a new phase in her life. Sam didn't like it, but then he was living in his own world. He refused to leave Fulton, but would still help support the kids at least.

Remembering she had not talked to Tina in a while, Niki had called her high school buddy who lived in Zion and shared her story about moving there. It was good talking to Tina. She encouraged Niki to come check things out.

"Come try the city on, girl. See how it fits," Tina said.

Her steps pretty much had already been ordered of the Lord when she heard in her spirit that she was moving to Zion. She had been given the order. Now she needed to get the vision, and a trip to visit her friend would accomplish just that. Once she had the vision, then it would not be long before it happened, because where God gives the vision, He also gives the provision. She just had to show up and get it.

Tina was happy to have Niki stay with her. They had always liked each other in school. Then they moved to different states after graduation. Niki went back to Fulton, while Tina went on to Dallas, New York, Chicago, and finally Zion. They ran into each other when they came home from college on breaks and holidays, exchanged phone numbers and addresses and had kept in touch over the years.

During Taj's spring break, he and Niki drove there with the sole purpose of securing an apartment. They were extremely prayed up. They had been very specific with God in their request about apartment size, location and environment.

Taj, a prayer warrior like his mother, remembered a joke she had told him about a mouse coming face to face with a lion. The mouse prayed "Lord, please let this be a Christian lion." The lion prayed, "Lord, thank you for this food," and ate the mouse. The mouse got exactly what he asked for. From then on, Taj became very specific in his prayers.

One specific request was that the apartment needed to be near Way Maker Ministries, because Niki knew she would be spending a lot of time there. Based on what she got from the TV broadcast, she knew that's where she had to be to make sure she heard clearly from God. She was staying close to her church in Fulton when she heard, in her spirit, to pack up and move.

"I know God is everywhere, Tina; but girl, I got to be hooked up to a dynamic ministry that is downright radical about the things of God. Have you ever heard of Way Maker Ministries?"

"Sure," Tina said. "It's not far from where I live."

"Girl, get outta here. See how God hooks stuff up?" Niki said, thrilled with the prospect that God was leading her to a place close to her girlfriend and her new church.

"Girl, if we just hang in there, it'll all work out. A few months ago, I was between a rock and a hard place with nowhere to go, no job, just stuck. Now with three words from God "Move to Zion" and Genesis 3:12 to stand on, it is taking all I got to keep from being overwhelmed from the excitement of what's about to happen," said Niki.

"I hear ya, girl. I can't wait to see you," said Tina.

Niki took Taj on her apartment hunting trip because he was growing into an excellent sounding board. He knew his mother so well and was very sensitive to her. In the beginning, it was out of survival. To avoid that quick backhand of hers, he had to figure her out to know what he could and couldn't get away with. But for the past few years, seeing all the stress and pressure she was under, because he loved her so much, he studied her to learn what he could do to relieve her of some of her burdens.

She loved to see *A*'s on their report cards, so he made sure he did well in school. She loved to laugh, and he loved it when she laughed, so he became quite the comedian, making her laugh so loud until her stomach hurt. He was the man now—he knew what she liked, and his job was to help her find it.

While riding around looking for apartments, Taj looked at the apartment book and said, "Turn right here, Mommy."

Niki turned and they ended up at a beautiful apartment complex. They got out, talked to the agent, toured the two, three, and three bedroom deluxe with the sunroom apartments. They were beautiful luxury apartments. Niki and Taj fell instantly in love with the three bedroom deluxe model. They went back into the rental office, completed the paperwork, and left believing God that they would be approved, even though the only means of income was child support. Not to worry, they could live off that and the proceeds from the sale of the house until she got a job. Besides she had skills. And, not only that, Zion was the land of opportunity. So they headed back to Fulton to tie up loose ends and to let the kids finish out the school year.

Niki called the rental agent every day from Fulton until she heard the good news.

"Your three bedroom deluxe has been approved, Mrs. Riley," said the rental agent.

"That's what I wanted to hear," said a relieved and confident Niki.

The move in date was set for June 7th, two days after school closed. She wasn't wasting any time hanging around Fulton.

Being led by the Holy Spirit, Niki had taken care of all business with the sale of the house, school and immunization records, bank accounts, movers, and everything else. She left no stone unturned. When it had been time to move, she was so ready. Everything had been taken care of down to the minutest detail. She was thorough, but she also depended solely on God to tell her what to do, when to do it, and how to do it. Her steps were ordered by God. She didn't move on anything until He gave her the green light to do so. Because of this, she was absolutely, positively, without a shadow of a doubt, sure that everything she did would work out. And it did every time. She had tapped into something. By hooking her human spirit up with the Holy Spirit, who knows everything there is to know about both her and God, Niki had tapped into all wisdom and all knowledge. This was the key to everything.

"I'm going out to get some breakfast. What kind of croissants do you want?" Niki asked the kids.

"I want bacon, egg, and cheese," said Maya.

"Me, too," said Taj. "Mom, can I have French toast sticks, too, cause I'm gonna need some extra strength with all the work we have to do today?" he asked, looking around.

Such a man. I am so proud of him, Niki thought. "Sure, baby, anything else? Let's see, hash browns, juice, and coffee for me, of course."

"That's it, Mommy," said Taj.

"I'll be right back. Put the chain on the door, and do not open it for anyone but me," she instructed.

Niki was back at the apartment in about 20 minutes, pulling her car in beside a couple who was just getting out.

Ooohhh, my neighbors, she thought, excited to find out what type of people she would be living around. Her experience had been that people in this town were very friendly and hospitable people.

The man was opening the door to an apartment downstairs, and she saw an ice breaking opportunity.

"Hello, I'm your new neighbor, Nicole Riley. Sorry for making so much

17

noise moving in last night. Hope we didn't disturb you too much," she said smiling from ear to ear, friendliness, excitement and joy gushing out.

They both just stared at her.

Niki's first thoughts were, *Why are they looking at me so serious? He's nice looking. She is not his wife. They think I'm crazy. Why aren't they at work? Mind your business, girl.*

The woman finally said in a serious tone, "Well, you had to move in."

The man said nothing, but just continued to stare at her.

Niki sensed this was not a good time to try to get into a conversation with these people.

"Well, have a nice day," she said, still grinning as she made her way up the stairs.

The kids were waiting, ready to throw down on some croissants.

"Let's eat!" she said.

They dug into the food. It tasted even better than usual to the hungry crew. They finished up and began the task of unpacking.

With the sounds from the radio to pump them up, the job was sweatless. They sang and danced as they worked all day long until they got tired or hungry.

The second day, Niki went to get some fast food. On her way in, another guy was coming out of the same apartment that she had seen the couple go into. He was smiling almost as much as Niki.

"Hi, how you doing?" he asked.

"Fine, thank you," Niki said smiling back trying to be as friendly as he appeared to be. She kept walking, although he hesitated like he wanted to meet this new neighbor. But Niki had hungry kids to feed, and this wasn't a good time for her, so she kept walking.

After they ate, they took a walk outside. It was a gorgeous day. The friendly neighbor was out washing his car. They exchanged hellos, but that was it. Niki and the kids strolled around the apartment complex. When they made their way back, he was still washing his car. They looked at each other and just smiled this time.

The apartment was beginning to look like home. Now that all the dishes were put away, they could give the fast food restaurants a break and fix a home cooked meal. The next morning, Niki went grocery shopping. She let the kids sleep and deadbolted them in. She had learned a long time ago, if at all possible, not to take the kids grocery shopping with her.

As she got in the car, she remembered she left the list on the counter. She had also learned a long time ago not to go shopping without a list. As she headed back towards the apartment, the friendly neighbor came out the door in shorts, T-shirt, and flip flops. He was clearly athletic, muscles everywhere looking like he didn't have a care in the world and nowhere to go. Niki wondered why he wasn't at work in the middle of a weekday. He looked young enough to live with his mama, but that wouldn't make sense 'cause she had seen the couple go in the same apartment the other day, and they all looked around the same age. *Mind your business, girl.*

"Beautiful day," she said.

"Sure is," he responded.

Niki wanted to ask him what he did for a living, but resisted the urge.

"Well, have a good one," she said as she ran up to the apartment to retrieve the list. When she came back out and got in the car, he was getting something out of his car. They made eye contact and smiled at each other. She was in the car and gone.

Niki spent $150 at the grocery store. That should hold them for at least a week. Yeah, right. She'll have to go back in a couple of days for milk, if nothing else. Taj drank it like it was water. Said he had to grow and milk was gonna make it happen.

When she got back, the kids were up and dressed. *Where's my smiling, friendly neighbor now?* His car was gone, so the idea she had had of him helping her take the groceries in went out the window. They made several trips to the car to get all the bags in. They put the groceries away and the last of the empty boxes in the car and took them to the dumpster.

While they were out, they drove to Way Maker Ministries to see what was happening. Tina had taken Niki there during their apartment hunting trip, so she knew exactly where it was. A few people were walking around the campus who appeared to be workers, but no services were going on so they left.

They continued to ride around, checking out the area to find where some needed establishments were located. They ended up on a highway close to the apartment with everything they could imagine. *This is great. The nearest mall is no more than 15 minutes from the apartment, and the movie theater even closer. We all love the movies. God has indeed led us to an excellent location.*

When they got home the girls went to their room—Mia to her dolls, Maya to write in her diary everything they had done today, and Taj went straight to his PlayStation.

Niki began dinner, a feast fit for a king, trying to offset some of the fast food they had overindulged in lately. The meal turned out wonderful. They ate so much until all they could do was fall out in the middle of the living room floor in front of the TV. They watched Kid's Cable that ran old reruns, from back when TV was wholesome, until they all fell asleep right where they lay. Niki was glad she had cable hooked up at the same time as she did the telephone.

19

Around 1 a.m. Niki woke up, threw some covers over everybody, and laid back down and slept until later that morning.

Niki spent the day on the phone, getting instructions to register the children for school. She found out that they needed to go to the health department and get their immunization records transferred onto the appropriate form in order to be allowed to enter the Zion Public School System. She gathered all the appropriate papers, and they headed out the door for the health department.

When they got outside, there was the smiling neighbor again.

What does he do? Niki's curiosity was getting the best of her.

"Hi, my name is Niki, this is my son Taj, and my daughters Mia and Maya," she said, sticking out her hand to him.

"I'm Randy. Nice to meet you."

Quickly thinking of something legitimate to say, Niki asked "Randy, do you know a good barber? Since we just moved here, I have to find one for my son."

"My roommate cuts hair."

"Really? Does he cut yours?" Niki asked checking out his haircut and concluding that if his roommate cut it, he was worth a try. She wondered if that cute guy with the girl was his roommate.

"Yes, he cut mine."

"Is he expensive and does he make house calls?" Niki asked jokingly. "I'm just kidding," she said. "What's his name?"

"Kevin," said Randy.

"Will you ask him if he will cut Taj's hair for me, please?"

"Sure, I'll ask him when he gets in tonight."

With that settled and noticing that the writing on his T-shirt said ZHS Football, and underneath that, Coaching Staff, she asked, "what's ZHS?"

"Zion High School where I teach," Randy answered.

Finally! Mystery solved. He's a teacher, and they have the summers off. That's why he's walking around here with nothing to do all day. Must be nice.

"What do you teach?" she asked.

"Math," he said.

"Heavy. You coach football, too?" Niki asked, trying to satisfy her curiosity.

"Yeah, I coach the wide receivers."

"Cool," Niki responded visibly impressed. She always thought that teachers and high school football coaches were the most important people in the world. She knew many young men who survived the streets only because of their high school football coaches. They replaced a lot of the absent fathers and helped get some of the players into college—a lot of them on scholarship. And teachers period, but especially high school math teachers, had the toughest jobs in the world. To motivate high school students to do well in math had to take a special type of individual.

"Where are y'all from?" asked Randy, just as curious about this woman with all these children.

"Virginia," answered Taj.

"Fulton, Virginia," said Mia, "and I want to go back."

"That's our cue to leave," said Niki. "See you later, Randy."

"Bye, nice meeting y'all," he said.

They got in the car, directions in hand, and headed to the health department. They all had to get a shot to be current on their immunizations and passed the seeing and hearing test with no problem. Finally, they left with all the required paperwork completed.

"That took forever. Let's go eat some leftovers," Niki said.

As they were walking into the apartment, Niki heard a door shut downstairs. She hesitated and looked to see who it was. She spotted the cute guy with a young boy walking to the car. She went in the apartment thinking, *He has a son about Taj's age.*

Later that night, there was a knock on the door. When she looked through the peephole, she saw the cute guy. He was a big guy, the linebacker type, thick neck and all. Between the basketball type—tall and thin—and the football type—shorter, muscular, and strong—she preferred the football type. Probably it was because she admired strength, and football types were, in her opinion, the stronger of the two.

"Hi, I'm Kevin. My roommate said your son needed a barber," he said without smiling when Niki opened the door.

So serious, thought Niki. "Hi, I'm Niki, and my son needs a haircut like yesterday," she said trying to loosen up this obviously tense guy.

"I have time now," Kevin said, still serious.

He doesn't mess around. "How much do you charge?" she asked.

"Six dollars."

"Okay, can you cut it here?" she asked thinking that was a good deal, hoping she got more than her money's worth in terms of quality.

"Sure, I'll go get my clippers. I'll be right back," he said as he turned and headed downstairs.

A few minutes later, upon entering her apartment Kevin said, "Wow! It's like night and day." He looked around, obviously impressed.

"What is?" asked Niki.

"Your apartment compared to ours," he said.

This was a refreshing touch of honesty, Niki thought. "Thanks, I guess," she said not wanting to sound presumptuous.

"No, this is beautiful. You got it really hooked up nice," Kevin said, still not smiling.

21

This is a serious guy. "Well, thank you very much. Where do you want to cut my son's hair?"

"The kitchen will be fine. The light is probably better in there than anywhere else."

"Okay. Taj!" she called.

Taj came out of his room and checked Kevin out as he stood beside his mother.

Putting her hand around his shoulder, she introduced them, "Taj, this is Kevin, our neighbor. He's a barber and came up to cut your hair."

Taj and Kevin solemnly shook hands.

"Hi," said Taj.

"Hey, man, how you doing?" Kevin responded.

"Fine," said Taj.

"Let's do this," said Kevin.

Taj sat in the chair in the kitchen as Kevin draped him with a sheet Niki had provided and began to set out his tools. As he combed through Taj's hair, Niki got out of the way. She could see them from across the breakfast bar as she organized some things in the sunroom. She couldn't help but notice how intense Kevin was. *He and his roommate must get along really well because they appear to be total opposites. Randy seems friendly, smiling all the time and Kevin seems so serious. I haven't seen him smile yet. Probably got a jacked-up grill,* she thought.

The haircut turned out pretty good, so Niki gave Kevin a ten dollar bill and told him to keep the change.

"Thanks a lot," he said, packing up his tools.

Taj was sweeping up his hair off the floor.

"Have you ever been to Way Maker Ministries?" Niki asked Kevin.

"No, where's that?" he asked.

"You don't know where Way Maker Ministries is as close as you live to it?" Niki said shocked, then hoping she hadn't offended him.

But Kevin was cool. He kept on with what he was doing.

"Nope," he said, never looking up.

"Well, you got to go. It is so blessed. I can't believe you haven't heard about this church right here in Zion." *He must not be from here,* she thought. "Where are you from?" she asked.

"Eden County, 30 minutes from here. Born and raised, all my life," he said.

Who could live right here and not know about the most awesome ministry on earth, she thought. *He must live with his head in the sand.* "That is utterly amazing. People are trying to get to this church from all over the world. One of my main reasons for coming here is to become a part of that ministry, and I can't wait to get there. What church do you go to?" she asked.

"Actually, I'm looking for one. I go with Randy to his church sometimes, but I haven't joined," he said.

"Well, why don't you come with us sometime? Just check it out since you're searching," she said.

"I'm game," said Kevin.

"Sunday?" Niki asked.

"Call me and remind me. I'll give you my number."

"Cool," she said.

Kevin wrote his phone number on a piece of paper, left it on the counter, and heading towards the door he said, "Goodnight, and thanks again for the tip."

"Have a blessed evening and thanks for making the house call."

That night Niki prayed, "Lord open Kevin's eyes to see and ears to hear. Prepare his heart to receive your Word so that he can grow in the things of God and be used by You. In Jesus' name, Amen."

CHAPTER 5

"Let's go!" yelled Niki. "I can't wait to get up on the inside of Way Maker Ministries. Come on, kids, get in the car."

The children, grabbing Bibles, pencils, pads, cute little purses, and lip gloss quickly filed out the door and got in the car.

"No wonder I didn't get an answer when I called downstairs to see if Kevin was going to church. Both of those brothers are gone. Neither one of their cars are out here. We'll catch them later; but right now, we got to go praise the Lord," Niki said as she pulled off.

"Buckle up," said Maya, the official Buckle Up Reminder Child.

Niki, seeming to always be in a hurry, was often halfway to where she was going before she remembered to buckle up. After seeing the crash dummies commercial and learning that you could get a ticket for not using your seatbelts, Maya assumed the responsibility for making sure her family rode in safety—buckled up, that is. Even if they were already buckled up, Maya said it anyway. It became a habit. Sometimes they needed the reminder; sometimes they didn't. But they got it whether they needed it or not. That was her job.

Her mom was pleased with them when they acted responsible. Maya, like her brother, sought to please her mom, mostly because she couldn't stand to be yelled at. There wasn't much she could do about her mom when she yelled for no reason, which happened from time to time. But she sure could do something to make sure she didn't yell directly at her with a good reason. So Maya, too, studied her mom to learn what it was that she had to do to keep her mother calm so that she had nothing to yell about.

Her mom liked people who took responsibility and "handled their business" without bothering her all the time. So whatever job Maya was assigned, she did it to the best of her ability and hoped and prayed that her mom would be pleased. If she wasn't pleased, it didn't matter how hard Maya worked, she got told.

"You call that cleaning up the kitchen? Is the kitchen floor a part of the kitchen? Is there still food on the kitchen floor? Do I have to say sweep the floor? Are you saving it for a special day to sweep the food off the floor? Did I say clean *half* the kitchen? When I say clean the kitchen, unless I specify an individual task, I mean clean the *whole* kitchen. That means wipe the grease off the stove, the crumbs off the table, and get the dirt off the floor. Don't let me have to say it again. Are there any questions?" her mother would state in a way that sent chills down Maya's spine. Maya hated those kinds of speeches from her mother. She learned a lot from them, but she hated them nonetheless. She learned exactly what it was her mother expected from her because Niki was so specific. She was also very responsible, and she accepted nothing less than her children showing responsibility. So they traveled to Way Maker Ministries all buckled up, arriving safe and sound.

When they pulled up on campus they were amazed at what they saw—a sea of cars, people galore trying to get into a couple of small buildings, an army of parking attendants, policemen directing traffic, and, not too far off, a huge unfinished dome of a building. There were lines and lines of people looking like they were waiting to buy tickets to a Michael Jackson concert. Anybody who didn't know what to expect would definitely think this is where it was happening. And they would be right. People were coming and going by the thousands.

When she had called earlier to find out what time service started, she was told 7 a.m., 9 a.m., and 11 a.m. on Sunday and 7 p.m. on Wednesday. She chose 9 a.m.

She was directed to park far away from the church. They walked across the yet to be paved dusty and rocky parking lot. This was not comfortable, but they really didn't notice. All they wanted to do was get to the happenings. The scene outside so excited each one of them that they could hardly wait to get on the inside. People were dressed up, dressed down, or uniformed like they were coming from or going to work. They saw nurses, truck drivers, waitresses, and even exterminators. A come-as-you-are church. Some said that's what they were, but this was the first one Niki had actually been to. *How absolutely liberating.*

She was directed to the children's church where she stood in line to sign the children into their classrooms. Once they were all signed in and delivered to the appropriate classes, she went over and got in another line to get into the sanctuary. The lines started outside each of the four entrances into the sanctuary, completely filled the hallway, went out all of the exit doors, and wrapped around the building. The scene was staggering. Niki couldn't think straight; she was so overwhelmed.

She followed the instructions that the ushers yelled at the worshippers and flowed right in with the crowd. She got pushed up through the door, down the hallway into the sanctuary and into a seat. The music was ushering them in. The crowd was praising and worshipping God.

She thought, *This is what the Bible means by entering into His gates with thanksgiving and into His courts with praise.* It all flowed so smoothly even though there were so many people. Being one in the spirit is the only way this could be pulled off. And flowing in obedience to the instructions of the ushers, of course.

Once settled in her seat, she looked around. As she took it all in, joy just came up and out of her in the form of tears, uncontrollable tears. She let them flow freely, laughing out loud, shouting HALLELUJAH! Lifting her hands in praise, clapping, rocking side to side, and stomping her feet, Niki had never ever felt this way before. She knew she was home. Watching the praise team, even though the songs were not familiar, she joined in the praise and worship. She cried some more and thanked the Lord for bringing her here. She was caught up.

After praise and worship was over and the congregation squeezed into their seats like sardines, Niki managed to regain control of herself and her tears. This must have been the norm because ushers were walking the isles with tissues and handed her a box to get what she needed. Wiping her eyes, she looked around her further. It hit her that this was the scene that she had been viewing every week on TV for the last few years. The revelation almost overwhelmed her, and she just rocked back and forth in her seat thanking Jesus.

After a few announcements and other preliminaries, she began to settle down. Then in came the pastor. She went into shock. She froze, eyes locked on him. She could not take her eyes off of him. Here in the same room with her was her link to everything her heart desired. She would close her eyes and re-member herself watching him on TV in Virginia, then open her eyes to see him right there in the flesh. She kept doing that until the tears flowed again as the revelation of where God had brought her from embraced her. She had been de-livered from between a rock and a hard place. Her future was brighter than ever.

When Pastor got up to preach, all the people disappeared in Niki's mind, and no one was there but her and Pastor. After a few minutes, Pastor disap-peared and only Niki and the Word of God that was coming out of his mouth were there. The Word had taken on a form of its own. It was no longer just a man standing there talking directly to Niki that began filling her, molding her, anointing her to do whatever God led her to do. The most powerful force there is, the Word of God itself, was ministering to her, pouring itself right into her spirit. It was the most awesome experience of her life.

After the message, Pastor was ushered out ahead of the crowd, and Niki watched him leave. She was speechless (which for Niki was something new) and felt numb. After the service, as the crowd pushed her out the door, she stag-gered toward the car. Then, realizing she had not picked up the children, she turned around, still dazed a bit, and headed to get in the Children's Ministry line.

She got it together somewhat while standing in line. By the time she signed the kids out, she was almost back to normal.

"How did you like church?" she asked the kids.

"It was the greatest, Mom," said Taj.

"We had fun," Mia jumped in. "We read our Bibles, watched videos, played games, and won prizes. Look at what I won," Mia said showing Niki a pad and pencil set. "Thanks for making me learn my books of the Bible, Mommy. I won because I knew the four gospels."

"I loved it too, Mommy," said Maya, the coolest of the three. It took a lot to impress Maya. If she loved it, that said a lot to Niki.

"How was your church, Mommy?" Maya asked.

"Awesome, awesome, awesome. I can't wait for the next time. I heard somebody say that the weekly Bible study is just like Sunday services. I got to see this. I can't wait 'til Wednesday," said Niki.

"Me either," the kids all said in unison as they walked to the car, not even noticing all the dust from the cars riding through the unpaved parking lot.

Getting something to eat and relaxing was next on their agenda. They went to a pancake restaurant because Niki was just too keyed up to cook. The food was pretty good. It did the trick, filled everybody up, and made them sleepy.

"I'm going to lay down for a couple of hours. What are you guys going to do?" Niki asked as she opened the door and they all filed into the apartment.

"I'm sleepy too," said Maya.

"Me too," Taj agreed.

The kids quickly changed clothes, found a comfortable spot and went straight to sleep: Maya on her bed, Taj on the sofa, and Mia on Niki's bed with her. Right as Niki was dozing off, the phone rang.

"Hello?"

"Hmm, hello. Hmm, this is Kevin. From downstairs."

"Hey, Kevin."

"I called to apologize for not going to church with y'all this morning. I went out of town and thought I would be back in time. But I just got back. Did y'all go?"

"We sure did."

"How was it?"

"Awesome, awesome, awesome. That's all I can say. We are all up here recuperating from it."

"Sounds exciting. Sorry I missed it," Kevin said.

"I will have to tell you all about it later," Niki replied.

"Okay. I just wanted to let you know I didn't intentionally not go. I'll holler at y'all later."

"Okay, Kevin, maybe later on this evening. I'll call you when we get ourselves together. Bye."

"Bye now."

CHAPTER 6

"Hello."

"Hello, may I speak to Kevin?"

"Speaking."

"Hey, whatcha doin'?" asked Niki.

"Watching the game. Who is this?" he asked.

"Niki, from upstairs. Have you guys eaten yet?" she asked.

"Naw, man. We're trying to decide what we're going to do about dinner now. Probably ride out for a hamburger or something," said Kevin.

"When's the last time you had a home cooked meal?" asked Niki.

"I couldn't even tell you," said Kevin.

"That's not good. Why don't y'all come up here for a home-cooked meal?" said Niki.

"Be right up," Kevin said as he hung up the phone.

Niki hung the phone up laughing. A few seconds later came a knock at the door. She saw Kevin through the peephole and opened the door, still laughing.

"It must have been a long while. Wash your hands and go on in the kitchen and help yourself. Where's Randy?"

"He was all into the game. On my way out the door, I told him you invited us to dinner, and he said bring him a plate back."

"Uh, uh. No way. This is not a take-out joint. Come, sit down, relax and enjoy, right here," Niki said establishing a standard. She was forever setting standards such as washing your hands in the bathroom and not in the kitchen sink. The kids called them rules, and they got on their nerves. But they obeyed each and every one of them because the alternative got on their nerves worse.

Kevin washed his hands in the kitchen sink and dried them on a paper towel. Niki let it go and forgave him this time, but made a mental note to be more specific the next time. She went into the kitchen behind Kevin, handing him a plate. As she took the top off of each pot, she gave him a tour of the menu.

"Your bread is here," she said uncovering perfect golden brown buttered rolls. Taking the top off a pot, she said, "These are the collard greens." She replaced the lid and uncovered the casserole dish. "Here's the macaroni and cheese." Removing the top to the roaster, she unveiled the most succulent looking beef short ribs, roasted to perfection with a beautiful barbecue sauce.

28

As she turned toward the refrigerator to take out the potato salad, she looked at Kevin who was standing behind her looking over her shoulder at the food. His tongue was literally hanging out of his mouth, eyes big as quarters. She burst out laughing. He looked so funny—cute, but funny. "Excuse me," she said, still laughing as she moved past him to the refrigerator. He took one step back to let her pass. She opened the door and took out a dish. She said, "And this is the potato salad."

"If it tastes half as good as it looks, I'm in for a treat. I mean it looks absolutely scrumptious," said Kevin.

"Well, go for it. We've all eaten, and you can just help yourself," said Niki.

"Thank you very, very much," he said, as he filled his plate.

Niki poured him a glass of lemonade and set it on the dining room table.

"If it's not hot enough, you can run your plate in the microwave for a couple of minutes," she said.

Tasting one of the ribs, Kevin threw his head back and shook it from side to side. "Hum, hum, hum. Lord have mercy. It's delicious just the way it is," he said, licking the barbeque sauce off his lips.

"Do you need anything else?" Niki asked.

"No, thank you. This is perfect. Sit down, relax 'cause you worked hard in this kitchen today," he said.

"All right," Niki said, taking a seat at the dining room table as she waited for Kevin to be seated. She couldn't wait to tell him about church. *He will be a captive audience, mouth full, can't interrupt like those people at home whom I tried to minister to. Just didn't want to hear it. But Kevin is going to want to hear this 'cause the experience was totally awesome, and I can't wait to share it with an adult.*

"This is so nice of you, Niki."

"No problem. We have plenty, and they'll be tired of it after tomorrow. One day of leftovers, then I'm throwing food away even though there's all those starving people in Ethiopia."

Kevin laughed, "If leftovers are a problem for you, please call downstairs so we can help you out."

She laughed. "The food is already blessed, but you might want to do your own praying," she said, sounding like a mother.

Niki hadn't had a lot of friendly adult conversation lately with being busy with the move and getting settled and everything. All her conversations with adults had been about taking care of some business. She felt good sitting here with this young man and actually began to relax for the first time in a long, long time.

Kevin blessed his food, but before he put the first bite in his mouth he said, "So tell me all about church."

29

Thankful for the opening, Niki delved in head first. "Kevin, it was the most awesome experience of my life," Niki said, full of genuine drama. "I was so caught up in it all. I haven't cried that much in I don't know how long. I needed that cry, too. I was able to release some stuff I had been carrying for a long time. It was so God.

"Okay, okay, I'll start at the beginning. First, when we got there, actual policemen, I mean uniformed guys, were directing traffic. It was awesome. Then they had parking lot attendants telling you exactly where to park. It was so organized. They got their stuff together. Thousands and thousands of people were coming and going. Lines and lines of people waiting to get in. You had to conclude that any place that has this many people standing in line has to have it going on.

"After I signed the kids into Children's Ministry, I finally made it into the sanctuary; and Kevin, I tell you what: heaven couldn't feel that much better. I thought I had gone there at one point. And the message was awesome. The pastor ministered to me. He said exactly what I needed to hear. But Pastor always did that, even on TV when I was still in Virginia. How he got my attention in the first place was I was training my mouth not to say anything I didn't want. I had learned to be a thermostat Christian as opposed to a thermometer Christian. Since the Bible says you can have what you say, you have to say only what you really want. Even if it doesn't look like it will ever happen, saying it will cause it to happen. So what you do is set your thermostat, you know, like you set the thermostat on the wall, to where you want the temperature to be. That's what we have to do in our lives: set our temperature where we want it to be with the words of our mouths. And eventually, just like the temperature eventually gets to where the thermostat says it should be, so it will be in our lives. That's different from the thermometer which tells us what the temperature currently is. That's what most of us do—complain about the way things are. Well, we know what it is. Why are we talking about it, keeping it going? No. Change the temperature on your thermometer by setting the thermostat with the words of your mouth to the way you want it to be. Keep on saying what you want and not what you have, and you will eventually and without a doubt have what you want.

"See, the Word of God says to call those things that are not as though they were, just like when it was all darkness and God said, 'Let there be light and there was light.' Hey, it works for us the same way, but in God's perfect timing. The only thing we have to do is maintain the faith no matter how long it takes. The Bible says to fight the good fight of faith. That's all we have to do. Jesus did the rest and until what we want becomes manifested, we just need to do one simple thing—maintain the faith no matter how long it takes. Don't get tired. The Bible says don't get weary in well doing because you will reap if you faint not. Get busy about the things of God while you are waiting for your blessing to manifest." She paused to take a breath and noticed Kevin staring at her.

"What?" she asked.

"Are you a preacher?" he asked sincerely.

Niki laughed again. "I do sound like one, don't I? I can surely preach when I want to, and I lost a lot of friends that way. I got caught up in what I was saying, and they weren't with me and just faded out of my life," Niki explained.

"Your friends left because you preached to them?" Kevin asked.

"They didn't exactly leave. I mean I love them and they love me, but some of them thought I had lost my mind when I first got saved. My family, too—my mama, daddy, and husband. But I was in it now. And all I wanted to do was talk about it. I guess I'm making the same mistake I made back then. Forgive me for rambling," she said.

"No, no. Please finish telling me. It is very interesting. I'm just tripping off how much you are into it," said Kevin.

Thankful for the audience, Niki continued, "Okay, then let me tell you about how I got hooked on Way Maker Ministries. I was out shopping one Saturday and ran into these people I knew. They asked me about my husband who I was upset with for one reason or another at the time. Now because I was training my mouth to only say good things, and there wasn't a good thing I could think of to say right then, I opted not to say anything about him, clenched my teeth, and went on to talk about something else. Well, the next morning, when I tuned in to the TV broadcast, right when Pastor appeared on the screen these were his exact words, 'You don't have to say anything for your bad attitude to come out. Somebody asks you about your husband and you say "pssshh," grind your teeth, and roll your eyes.' Kevin, I sat straight up in the bed. He did it exactly like I had done it the day before. It blew my mind. I got mad when the broadcast went off. I couldn't wait for the next week's show.

"Then the next week, the same thing. Told me all my business. Busted me down to the bone to the point where my husband wasn't looking so bad anymore now that *my* sins were being exposed. The sick part was I didn't think anything was wrong with me because my sins were not blatant. I was Sister Super Christian, you understand; I did no wrong. And I was alienating everyone around me trying to be Miss Perfect. Then, to add insult to injury, I would tell my family and friends what they should and shouldn't be doing, calling out their sins. That's the part they couldn't take. I got on my dad for drinking, my friends for fornicating, my cousins for using drugs, my husband for breathing. Pastor made me see just how 'holier than thou' I had become. When I realized I had a lot of work to do on myself, I knew I needed to get out of that environment because it was just getting too hard. And there was no future there, so no real reason for us to stay. That's when God released me to leave and here I am."

"Wow," Kevin said, mouth full with his last bite, clearly fascinated by Niki's story.

"So, about the church," said Niki, "I can't remember it all to give the experience justice. You are just going to have to experience it for yourself."

"I can see that," he said.

"Would you like some more to eat?" she asked.

"Noooo, no thank you. That was delicious. I honestly can't remember the last time I had a meal that good," he complimented her.

"Thank you, sir," Niki said, almost blushing at the compliment. "We got some ice cream, vanilla."

"Daaagggg, you go all out, don't you? Maybe later; I'm just too stuffed to eat another bite," said Kevin.

She nodded and smiled, feeling real relaxed and good about her new friend. "So what do you do?"

"Teach. Actually, I'm substituting until I land a provisional contract while I pursue my teaching certification. My degree is in business, and I have to finish up some course work in order to get certified."

"Is Randy certified?" asked Niki seizing the opportunity to learn more about her neighbors.

"Randy was a straight math major. Since he's a math teacher, he had all the courses he needed to get certified," explained Kevin.

"Oh, I see," said Niki.

"What was your major?" asked Kevin, assuming she had gone to college.

"Accounting."

"I hated accounting," said Kevin.

"Most people do," said Niki. "That's why we can always find work."

"Where do you work now?" he asked.

"I don't. I got my resumé package ready to take over to the church tomorrow. But I don't want to work right now. Maybe after school starts. I need to be here for the kids, to make sure they are settling in all right. Know what I mean?" Niki said.

"Sure and you can do that with an accounting degree. You're in demand," said Kevin.

"And so are you—young, strong, intelligent black man in the classroom. That's exactly what our children need to see."

"True. And I love it," Kevin said.

"What grade do you teach?" asked Niki.

"I've been all over. I want to teach on the high school level and help get kids ready for college. Right now, I'm teaching at the elementary school. They are so special at that age, and I understand the importance of a good strong influence in their lives at this critical time. See, I had an interesting upbringing."

"Really?" Niki asked wanting to know what was interesting about Kevin's upbringing.

"My mom died when I was in elementary school. I never knew my dad, and my grandmother raised my sister and me. She did the best she could. We lacked for some things, but we knew she loved us and that got me through. I had football as an escape route. I took my frustrations out on the field, and that's what got me into college. I'm the only one in my family who ever went to college. I always knew God had his hand on me. I can't preach like you, but I know God loves me and has always taken care of me. I just do the best I can do and trust Him the rest of the way," said Kevin.

"You're preaching now. You don't have to quote scripture and verse to be preaching," said Niki.

"Amen, then," said Kevin. "So you want to work at the church? What do you want to do, accounting?"

"Not necessarily. Whatever they need me to do. I've been out there in the work force for a number of years. I got some skills. So I'm not concerned about work, but I will get my resumé on file there, so when I'm ready I'll be one step ahead," she said. Switching gears on him she asked, "Are you ready for that ice cream?"

"Actually, I'm still full," he said, "but I'll take a raincheck. I'm gonna get on back downstairs. Thanks again for dinner. I'm gonna go and mess with Randy now and tell him he missed it."

"Glad you enjoyed it. See you later," she said, walking him to the door.

Downstairs, Randy was ending a phone conversation when Kevin walked in the door rubbing his stomach.

"Man, you missed it. Homegirl can throw down," Kevin said super-hyped up.

"Where's my plate then?" Randy asked.

"Man, she said this ain't no take-out restaurant. You want something to eat at her crib, you come sit down up there and eat it. She don't be buying no food to distribute to the neighborhood. What's wrong with you, man?" Kevin said picking on Randy.

"What you eat, man? I know your greedy butt tore it up," asked Randy.

"Man, she had greens, macaroni and cheese, potato salad, hot buttered rolls and beef ribs, man, fell off the bones. Lemonade and vanilla ice cream," Kevin overemphasized to rub it in.

Randy stood up. "I'm going up there," Randy said heading towards the door.

"Man, come back here, man. You blew it. The kitchen is closed. Leave that woman alone. You just missed that one. You're gonna have to wait for the next one," Kevin said with a protective warning tone.

"Dag, man. Then shut up about what you ate. I'm going to get me some wings. Dag," Randy said as he left.

CHAPTER 7

"Mom, we're going to need some more milk today," said Taj.

"Boy, I'm going to buy you a cow for your birthday," Niki responded. "After breakfast, I am going to run up to the church to drop off my paperwork in personnel. I heard they have a whole personnel department. You all stay here and chill, and I'll be back as soon as I can, okay?"

"Sure, Mom. We'll be okay," said Taj.

"Yeah, take your time," Maya agreed.

"You all are so responsible. I really appreciate how well you've been behaving. You're the most precious darlings in the world, and I thank God for blessing me with you," praised Niki.

They all just grinned at their mother's kind and loving words.

Niki went into her room and got dressed. She wasn't sure what to put on. She decided on a long, beige dress with beige, brown, and olive flowers with a lightweight beige jacket to dress it up a bit, but not too much, and some flat olive shoes. Her makeup was light and attitude perfect. Her short low-maintenance haircut was a blessing at times like these when she wanted to look sharp and stylish without a lot of work. She needed a drastic change for her new venture. If she had not told Antonio to cut her long mane off before she left Virginia, she would have a tired ponytail right about now. *Oh, Antonio, what am I going to do without you?* she wondered. Her hair loved Antonio. He had it trained to cooperate with his every whim. She just allowed him to have his way with her hair because over the eight years she had been going to him she had always left his chair completely satisfied. He would be hard to replace.

She looked ready to conquer the world. Upon arriving at the church, she went to the front desk and informed the receptionist that she was there to deliver her resumé to the personnel director. Just then a woman walked in the door and stood beside Niki and began talking to the receptionist.

"Any messages for personnel, Sister Tonya?" the woman asked.

"No, Sister Erica," said Tonya.

An alert Niki zeroed in on Sister Erica.

Extending her hand Niki said, "Hello Sister Erica. My name is Nicole Riley."

Sister Erica shook Niki's hand.

"Hello, Sister Nicole," she said.

Niki saw an opening.

"I am an accountant with 15 years of experience. I just moved here from Fulton, Virginia, and am very interested in working here at the church. I have been saved and living for Jesus for six years. This is my resumé and letters of recommendations from the ministers of my church in Virginia," Niki said handing her the package.

Sister Erica was smiling as she took the package. Niki had made a good first impression.

"Walk with me to my office," she said.

"Thank you," Niki said overjoyed from the favor she was being shown.

They walked down the hall to personnel and entered Sister Erica's nice plush office.

Wow, looks just like corporate America, Niki thought.

"Have a seat," Sister Erica said as she retrieved an employment application from the files.

Handing it to Niki on a clipboard, she said, "Take a few minutes to complete this application, and I'll be right back."

"Thank you," said Niki, feeling really welcome.

Sister Erica left Niki to complete the application. When she returned, Niki handed her the completed form. Sister Erica scanned it for accuracy and presentation as she sat down. As everything appeared to be in order, she looked directly into Niki's eyes.

"So tell me about yourself," she said.

Wow, Niki thought, am I being interviewed? This is sudden. I had better be totally professional in case I am. But what do church people want?

She knew what corporate America wanted and could handle herself in a secular interview, all business and no personal information. Not real personal anyway. But this was different: it was sudden; and before she panicked, she decided to let the Holy Spirit lead. So she relaxed, sat back, let the peace of God overtake her and began.

"Well, my children and I just moved here from Fulton, Virginia. Not to sound redundant, my resumé clearly states my education and experience. However, three years ago I made the decision to become a housewife and start my own business doing something I like doing so that I could be home with my children. During that time, I did a lot of volunteer work at my church and decided that when I reentered the work force, I wanted to work for the Lord, which is why I am seeking employment here."

Niki hesitated before going on, contemplating if she should get any more personal. She felt an urging to do so. Sister Erica was very patient, sensing that she had more to say or was gathering her thoughts. She quietly gave Niki all the time she needed and really made Niki feel comfortable. So Niki proceeded.

"I left my husband in Virginia to move here because he is having a challenge with drugs," she said being careful to use the proper Christian lingo. *Christians don't have problems, just challenges. Don't give the devil any credit for causing us problems. Challenges make us better. Yeah, that's it.*

She continued, "After so many years, it wasn't getting any better; so I asked the Lord to deliver me from the situation. I have been watching the Way Maker Ministries broadcast for years. I've always felt like this is my second church home. I asked God to bring me here, and He did. I am so thankful to be here and I am looking forward to getting involved," said Niki.

Sister Erica interjected, "Before you can function in any of the ministries, you must complete a new members class. It consists of 15 individual classes. If you plan to get involved, you need to get the classes started right away," said Sister Erica.

Fifteen weeks! "Do you go through the whole Bible?"

"No, the classes are designed to teach you what the Bible says about our vision and mission to make sure you are in agreement with this church. If you find that there is something you don't agree with and are not able to line up with it, then you will find out in class, and you can reevaluate if this is the place where you are supposed to be. Take tithing for instance. Pastor teaches the class on tithing. He proves beyond the shadow of a doubt, by the Scriptures, that tithing is of God. Whoever can't get with that may not want to be here after that class. And it's mandatory that you tithe to be on staff," she explained.

"No problem. I got a revelation on tithing a long, long time ago. I live off my tithe. That's why I can't even be concerned about a job or money because my relationship with the Lord is solid, and it was firmly established when I started paying that ten percent. He met all my needs over and above all I could ask or think. I have faith that the more I give, the more I will receive," said Niki feeling a preach coming on and stopping herself. "So how do I sign up for classes?" she asked.

"New members classes meet on Thursdays at 7:00 p.m. Just come and get started. They are individual classes and are ongoing so you can start with any one of them," said Sister Erica.

"Great. I'll be there Thursday," said Niki.

Sister Erica, having a good feeling about this young lady, changed the subject. "How many children do you have?" she asked.

"I have three—one son and two daughters. My son, Taj is twelve. Maya is eleven, and Mia is six. Do you have any children?" Niki asked, then wondered if she should have since this could be an interview. But she felt good talking to this woman.

"No children, lots of nieces and nephews though. I lost a six-year-old son to a drunk driver five years ago. Never could bring myself to have any more," Erica revealed.

Niki couldn't imagine anything like that happening to Taj. She sent up a quick prayer declaring that his life was redeemed from destruction and dispatched even more angels to protect all of her children in all of their ways all the days of their lives. Her heart went out to Sister Erica.

"I can't even imagine what you went through," said Niki.

"Hell. My marriage suffered, ending in divorce, and I was driven straight to Jesus. Been here ever since. So I can empathize with you having gone through marital challenges," said Erica.

"How are you doing now?" Niki asked, full of genuine concern for this woman she was being drawn to.

Erica, sensing Niki's sincere concern along with a refreshing, open honesty, said, "You know, we probably need to get together after work and talk. Where do you live?"

"I live in Gardenpatch apartments. Do you know where they are?"

"Right around the corner from my house. I'm talking walking distance," said Erica.

"No way!" said Niki.

"Yes way," said Erica. "What are you doing this evening?"

"Nothing. Please come by and meet the kids. Have dinner with us," Niki bribed.

"Ohhh, you're talking my language now. And I would love to meet the kids. What's a good time?" asked Erica.

"Any time. What's good for you?" asked Niki.

"Well, I get off at five o'clock. I'll go home and change and come around six thirty, seven o'clock," Erica calculated.

"Perfect. What do you like to eat?" asked Niki.

"Anything."

They both laughed.

Sister Erica got up, professionalism back on, and Niki rose with her, following her lead.

Sister Erica extended her hand, "I will read the paperwork you have submitted, and you will be contacted should there be a match between your qualifications and the needs of the ministry. If there is not a match, then your resumé and application will be kept on file. Should a match become available, you will be contacted to see if you are still interested, and if so, you will not have to resubmit an application, just update. It has been a pleasure talking to you. And I'll see you this evening. Is this your correct address and phone number here on your resumé?"

"That's it, and thank you so much for taking the time to talk to me. I just knew God was leading me to the right place. I'll see you later," said Niki.

They shook hands, both realizing that this was the beginning of a new and beautiful friendship.

CHAPTER 8

"We have to clean this place up; we're having company," said Niki loud, happy, and excited.

"Who? Kevin?" asked Taj hopefully.

"No, Sister Erica."

"Who is Sister Erica?" asked Maya.

"She is the person who does the hiring at Way Maker Ministries. Thank you, Father, that I walk in Your favor and Your power and Your comfort. And she's coming here, Hallelujah!" shouted Niki.

"Why?" asked Taj

"Well, because as we were talking, I seriously believe that God was hooking us up. I felt really connected to her, real comfortable like we have been knowing each other for years. We talked about some of everything," said Niki.

"Mom, that's not unusual for you. You talk to anybody about anything all the time. We should know. We're the ones who have to stand around and wait for you, especially when you run into people you know in the mall and start talking about Jesus. We start looking for a place to sit down," said Taj.

"Yeah, Mommy, you can go, girl," said Maya.

"Watch your mouths now," Niki said jokingly because she knew it was true. Her kids knew her so well. And she did talk too much from time to time, off on a tangent, and never knew she had lost the listener a long time ago.

Niki decided to cook something special for her special guest.

"I'll be right back. I'm going to run to the grocery store. Chain and deadbolt the door, Taj."

"Okay, Mom."

Niki was quite the little cook when she wanted to be. She decided on chicken since every time she turned around, somebody was claiming they don't eat red meat. Then she would see them eating a burger. *Could have been a turkey burger; shut up, girl.*

Taj's specialty was baked chicken. Granddaddy had taught him well. So she bought two chickens, rice, and string beans. She bought a cake to go with the ice cream. And lemonade was the universal drink.

She managed all the grocery bags herself in one trip.

"Taj, hook the chickens up, man."

"Cool, Mom! You're going to let me cook for your friend? You really do like my cooking."

"Was there ever any doubt? Truth be told, you do a better job than me with those chickens. Granddaddy rubbed off on you. We have to call them tonight, too. Better yet, I'll call them tomorrow and let them know how nice these people are and about dinner tonight."

"Oh, Granddaddy called while you were at the store," said Taj.

"Oh, Lord. Did he have a conniption fit 'cause I left you here alone?" asked Niki.

"Of course he did. I told him we were all locked in like Fort Knox, and you would be back in a few minutes. I tried to cover for you," explained Taj while gathering together all of the ingredients for his chicken.

"Did it work?" she asked.

"Of course not. But don't worry, Mom. I'll tell the judge you're not an unfit mother," Taj joked, messing with her.

Niki laughed at her comedic son, wondering which one of her parents had threatened to turn her in, then deciding it must have been her dad. "He'll get over it," she said.

"He said they might be down next weekend, if it's okay with you," said Taj.

"Of course it's okay with me. I'm surprised they haven't shown up yet."

"He said he wanted to make sure we were all settled in first before they came to visit. Didn't want to get in the way."

"I do miss them, and I'm ready to see them now." Niki was smiling thinking about her parents. They are great parents in spite of everything. She was real blessed to have them. She was smiling because she knew now that with the distance between them, their relationship would eventually be much better than it was when they were living right in the same city. She just needed a little space, that's all.

After the chickens were done soaking in salt water, Taj began his masterpiece. Niki got out of his way until the chickens were in the oven.

"I'm done," yelled Taj.

"Thanks, baby."

They straightened up the apartment, dusting, vacuuming, making sure everything was in place. Niki put the vegetables on. She planned to pop the bread in the oven when Erica arrived so it would be good and hot. The phone rang.

"Hello," answered Taj.

"Mom, telephone," he called.

"Hello," said Niki.

"Hi, this is Erica. I'm on my way, okay?"

"Sure. Come on," said Niki, excited about her guest. Erica was just

39

about the nicest person Niki had ever met—friendly, open, and honest. *How refreshing.*

Ten minutes later, Erica was knocking on the door. Niki looked through the peephole to make sure, then opened the door.

"Hello, Sister Erica, come on in. Mi casa is your casa," Niki said speaking Spanglish.

"Ooooh, it smells good in here," said Erica.

As they walked into the apartment, Niki led her to the kitchen where Taj was basting his chickens. They were ready; he was just putting the finishing touches on them, looking very much like a seasoned, midget chef minus the hat.

"Sister Erica, this is Taj, my oldest and only son. Taj, this is Sister Erica, from Way Maker Ministries."

Taj, putting down the spoon and wiping his hands, went over and shook Erica's hand. "Nice to meet you," he said.

"Very nice to meet you, too, Taj," Erica said smiling, thinking this was the most adorable thing she had ever seen, a little polite, child chef basting chicken.

"Mia, Maya, come here," called Niki.

The girls came out of their room and stood facing Erica, waiting to be introduced. Niki stood behind Maya with both hands on her shoulders and said, "This is my big girl, Maya." Moving over to Mia and putting her hands on her shoulders, she said, "And this is my little girl, Mia."

The girls were smiling.

"Girls, this is Sister Erica."

"Hello, Sister Erica," they sang together.

"Well, aren't you adorable. Little princesses. How are you?" Erica said smiling down at them.

"Fine," they sang some more.

"Well, it is a pleasure to meet all of you," Erica said.

"It's a pleasure to meet you, too, Sister Erica," all three children sang.

"Awwww, how sweet," said Erica genuinely moved by the way Niki had raised them. She had instantly fallen in love with all three children, especially Taj.

"I'll call you when dinner is ready," Niki said, dismissing the children. Turning to Erica, she said, "I'm going to put the rolls in the oven. We should be ready to eat in about 15 minutes. Just make yourself at home."

Looking around, Erica said, "Girl, your apartment is hooked! I love your mirrors."

"Thanks. They just seem to open things up for me, I don't know," said Niki as she put the bread in the oven.

They sat at the dining room table so Niki could jump up and check on the bread every few minutes. They had to be perfect for Niki to serve them.

"Did you work in personnel before you came to the church?" asked Niki.

"I've always been in personnel. I'm a people person, I guess," said Erica.

"I've always been in accounting. I'm a numbers person, I guess," said Niki. They both laughed.

"Where have you been since you moved here to Zion?" asked Erica.

"Besides church, to the grocery store and health department," answered Niki.

"Oh, I have to take you out," said Erica.

"Please do," she said sounding desperate.

"Do you know anybody here?" Erica asked.

"Yeah, an old school buddy from back home that I stayed with on my apartment hunting trip. She has never been to Way Maker Ministries and isn't interested in going either. She brought me though, and I am most grateful for that," Niki said getting up. "I'm just going to check on the bread." Looking in the oven she said, "A few more minutes." She got out the plates, glasses, and silverware.

"Need any help?" asked Erica.

"You want to butter the rolls?" asked Niki.

"Okay, where's the bathroom so I can wash my hands?" asked Erica.

Niki thought, *I really like her. She knows the rules.* "Right around that corner," Niki said pointing towards the hallway.

She took the bread out of the oven, got the butter out of the refrigerator, grabbed a butter knife, and set them all on the table. Erica buttered the rolls as Niki set the food on the table. Once the table was spread, she called the kids.

"Wash your hands and come eat!"

They all took their places at the dinner table.

"Bless the food, Taj," said Niki.

"Dear Lord, thank you for this food. We bless it and receive it with thanksgiving for it is sanctified by the Word of God in this prayer. In Jesus' name we pray. Amen," prayed Taj.

"Amen," agreed Erica visibly impressed with the young man's ability to pray the Word of God. *Good thing the Lord healed me of all my pain and feeling of loss that followed Emmanuel's death, because I might try and steal Taj away from Niki.*

As they fixed their plates and ate, Erica told them about the church and the Children's Ministry. The kids loved her instantly. She told Niki that if she ever needed a break, she would be happy to watch the kids. She could tell that Niki spent a lot of time with them, training them in the things of God.

"So what grade are you going to be in when school starts?" asked Erica.

"I'm going to be in seventh grade," said Taj.

"I'm going to be in sixth," said Maya.

"Second grade," said Mia.

"That's wonderful. So what kind of grades do you get?" Erica asked, sensing their intelligence.

"All *A*'s because Mommy doesn't want us to bring *B*'s in the house," said Maya.

Erica looked at Niki. "Why am I not surprised?" she asked.

"Got to keep the standards high," said Niki.

"That's our mom," said Maya, "but we love her."

They all laughed.

After they finished eating, the kids went to watch The Good Old Days Channel. Their favorite oldie was coming on in five minutes. Erica helped Niki clear the table, load the dishwasher, and clean up the kitchen. When they finished, they joined the kids who were falling out laughing at something on TV.

"TV was great back then. Now, there's no telling what you might see come across the tube. Things have been getting so bad, it makes you wonder how long the Lord will tarry until He comes to take us home." said Erica.

"That's for sure. Our TV pretty much stays on The Good Old Days Channel. It's the safest thing I've found for them to watch," said Niki.

Erica was feeling right at home, laughing with the kids at the old black and white TV show. "You guys want to hang out tomorrow? Maybe ride to the mall or something?" she asked

"Yeah," said Taj.

"The mall. Yes!" cried Maya.

"Sure," answered Niki ready to do something different besides taking care of business.

"Then I'll come by about the same time. Got to do my hanging out on Monday and Tuesday because something is normally going on at the church Wednesday through Friday," Erica said.

"Cool. We'll be ready to hang out," said Niki. "And I can't wait to get involved at the church. I'm going to start those classes this week."

"And you'll get blessed. You'll learn a lot, too. Real deep, very informative. Some people take them lightly and don't pass the test," said Erica.

"What test?"

"Oh, I didn't tell you. Yeah, girl, a test that you must pass to graduate," said Erica.

"Graduate?"

"I'm telling you, it's serious. You have commencement exercises and graduation pictures in your cap and gown holding your certificate of completion. It's a big deal. Pastor imparts the vision to you during the ceremony. You have a reception afterwards where all the ministries try to recruit you. It's blessed," Erica explained.

"Oh wow, I'm real excited now!"

"You're in for a treat—a lot of work—but it's all good," said Erica. Getting up and stretching, she said, "I'll call you tomorrow, make sure everything is still on. After that good meal I'm ready to get comfortable and get in my bed, know what I mean?"

"Yes, ma'am. Hope you enjoyed it," said Niki.

"Oh, girl. I don't know when was the last time I've felt this good, ate this good, relaxed and laughed this much. I have thoroughly enjoyed my evening. Thanks for inviting me, and I just love the kids," Erica said, walking to the door.

"Thank you so much for coming. We have really enjoyed your company. I thank God for you."

Niki walked Erica to the car. Kevin was pulling up as they were coming down the stairs.

"God has surrounded me with some good folk. That guy getting out of the car is my neighbor and Taj's new barber. Makes house calls and cheap. Real nice, him and his roommate," said Niki.

"He's kinda cute," said Erica.

"That's what I thought. He's young, got a son, got a girlfriend, and I got a husband. Don't know what I'm going to do with my husband, but I got one," laughed Niki.

"You'll know what to do when it's time to do something," said Erica.

"I can't wait," said Niki.

They both laughed as Kevin approached.

"Evening, ladies," he spoke.

"Good evening, Kevin. This is Sister Erica, my friend from Way Maker Ministries. Sister Erica, this is my neighbor Kevin," Niki said introducing her two newest best friends.

They shook hands.

"Nice to meet you," said Erica.

"Same here," he said.

"I'll talk to you tomorrow, Niki. Good night," said Erica.

"Bye. Get home safe," said Niki.

Kevin was still standing there as Niki watched Erica get in her car and pull off. If Niki was watching out for Erica, then Kevin was watching out for Niki.

She turned to him, "So how was your day?"

"Good, and yours?" he responded.

"Wonderful. I met a new friend, Sister Erica, who just so happens to be in a high place. But I know it's on me."

"Huh?" Kevin said, not following her.

"See, Sister Erica is personnel director at the church. Remember, I told you just yesterday that I wanted to work at the church. Well, that had to be God to hook us up. I met her today, and we hit it right off. Nobody but God."

"Hey, I believe you, Niki, and I'm happy for you. It's good to have friends in high places. Look, I was wondering if I could share something with you?" he asked.

"What?" asked Niki.

"It's a business opportunity. Something you can do while you are waiting for your job to come through," he explained.

Niki had heard them all, had seen them all, had tried them all.

"Kevin what are you selling?"

Being the open, honest, not-to-beat-around-the-bush type, he said, "Knives."

"Kutright?" asked Niki.

"How did you know that?" Kevin asked surprised.

"Got some. They have a lifetime warranty, right?"

"Right."

"Then I don't need any more."

"Well, could you do me a favor when you have some time and just listen to my presentation? I'm trying to perfect it, and that only comes from doing it. I can do it in front of the mirror, but I need some constructive criticism, you know, some feedback. If you could be my audience one day this week, that would be great," admonished Kevin.

"How long does your presentation take?" asked Niki.

"No more than 30 minutes with all the demonstrations. But I can make it shorter," he said.

"What time do you get home?" she asked.

"Around 4:30-5:00," he answered.

"Well, we're riding out with Sister Erica tomorrow, and we'll be tied up for the rest of the week. If not before we leave tomorrow, then I'll have to let you know. But I'll be happy to be your audience," she said.

"That's fine. Just let me know when you're available. Look, I really appreciate this."

"No problem. Hey, Kevin, when are you going to let your son play with Taj?"

"Son? I don't have a son," said Kevin.

Ooops. That's what you get for jumping to conclusions. You are going to have to work on that, girl. Get the facts straight before you open your big mouth. The kids just told you that you talk all the time.

"Oh, I'm sorry, I saw a little boy about Taj's age with you the other day and just assumed he was your son. I should know better than to assume," said Niki.

"Oh, that was my nephew, Rashad. Yeah, I get him from time to time to give my sister a break," Kevin clarified.

Well that explains that. I even gave that misinformation to Erica. I need to shut up for real. Wonder where his girlfriend is? I haven't seen her since that first day. Girl, mind you own business.

CHAPTER 9

During a Way Maker Ministries administrative meeting, the decision was made to separate the outreach part from the local church part of the ministry. Everything had been handled as one big operation up until this point. The growth of the ministry was overwhelming the current staff. No one could have foreseen this rapid growth. Way Maker Ministries was known as one of the fastest growing churches in the nation. Before the excellence of the ministry was compromised, an executive decision had to be made. It was clear that these two ministries were distinct and unique and should be separated administratively. Outreach needed its own staff, its own administrator, its own accountant.

DING! DING! DING! Alarms went off in Erica's head as she sat in the strategic planning meeting to determine how to go about affecting this change. She had read Niki's paperwork yesterday and was very impressed. However, there was no position at the ministry that required her expertise yesterday. But today, a new day, the day that the Lord had made, full of new mercies, this day there was a position that matched Niki's paperwork. *She is clearly walking in the favor of God,* Erica thought.

She had to be cool. She was so excited for Niki, but being in her position, there was nothing she could do for her friend. Niki was completely on her own. All Erica could do was pray, which had proven in the past to be more than enough. She couldn't wait to get back to the office to call Niki.

"That's it. Let's get to work," said Pastor, and the meeting was adjourned.

Erica all but ran back to her office. She picked up the phone and dialed Niki's number.

"Hello," answered Niki.

"Girl, your Daddy loves you."

"What, what?" Niki said, recognizing Erica's voice, excitement bubbling up on the inside just from those few little words from Erica. "What?" she yelled.

"I just got out of a meeting, and I have been instructed to advertise for several new jobs and guess what one of them is?"

"What, what?"

"Outreach Accountant."

"Accountant, are you serious? I'm an accountant. Have been one forever."

"I know, I know. But, girl, you are completely on your own. You my sister and I love you, but I can't raise one little pinky finger to help you," said Erica.

"Girl, I got this. God ain't hardly brought me this far to leave me," said Niki.

"Just know you are on your own. All I can do is pray. I will submit the strongest resumés and applications received to the Controller, and you pray that yours is in there. But I can tell you this: You're looking good so far. I mean, I haven't advertised yet, but as far as resumés go, you're looking real good. It's going to take quite a bit to top what you submitted. I got your back in prayer. That's my limit," said Erica.

"Don't worry, I got it, in prayer and every other way. Tell me, did you know about this position yesterday?" asked Niki.

"That's why I'm so excited. It didn't exist yesterday. Do you see God in this?" asked Erica.

"Clear as day. What do I need to do?" asked Niki.

"Nothing. I have your paperwork, and the job hasn't even been advertised. Just wait for your interview. You might want to go on and knock those new member classes out ASAP," said Erica.

"Glory be to God! Thanks, Sis. See you this evening. I got to go pray," said Niki.

"Bye," said Erica.

When Niki hung up the phone, she called the kids. "We got to pray. God has created a position for me at the church. We got to pray so the devil can't steal it from me. Pray that I have the position of outreach accountant that God created just for me and can't nobody have it but me because I am the only one called, anointed, and appointed to that position in Jesus' Name." They prayed together and individually and in tongues pretty much all day as they went about their normal routine.

Around 4:30, there was a knock at the door. Niki looked through the peephole. It was Kevin. She opened the door.

"Hey. Are you busy?" he asked.

"Busy praying. Come in. I got to tell you this and get you to stand in agreement with me," she said.

He followed her into the apartment.

"Didn't I tell you I was going to work at the church?" she asked.

"Yes," he remembered.

"Well, I went up there and submitted my paperwork, and there wasn't a position that matched my qualifications. But now, a newly created position is being advertised. My job. Accountant. God brought me here for that job. Now I need you to stand in agreement with me that that is my job until I start working. It has to be advertised, and others have to be given the opportunity to apply. But when it's all said and done, we shall see who ends up in that position," said Niki.

"Will that be you?" asked Kevin.

"That will be me," she answered, confidence in what God was doing in her life oozing out of her.

"You know it, huh?" Kevin asked.

"Like I know my name. It's called 'faith.' Do you agree with me?"

"Heck, yeah. As positive of an influence as you are, you deserve it," Kevin said, setting himself in agreement.

"It's a done deal then. So did you come up to do your presentation?" she asked.

"Do you have time now?"

"Sure, Erica won't be here 'til around 6:30."

"Cool. I'm gonna run down and get my material. Be right back."

"Just come on in. I'll leave the door unlocked."

"Okay."

"Taj! Maya! Come in here," called Niki.

Mia was outside playing at the playground with some neighborhood kids she had met.

"Kevin wants to do a presentation, and he needs an audience. Would you mind listening to him with me?"

"Okay," Taj said. He liked Kevin. He liked football, and Kevin knew a whole lot about football.

They all sat on the sofa. Kevin came right on in, didn't knock or anything.

He sure follows directions well, thought Niki.

He looked at the three of them sitting on the sofa.

"Wow, a real live audience. Hope I don't get stage fright."

They laughed.

As he sat up his materials on the coffee table, they paid close attention. Kevin went through his presentation like a professional. He had a nice presenter's voice so he kept their attention. He had a lot of personality, character, and charm, not like that first night he had come up to cut Taj's hair. That reminded Niki to check out his teeth.

Humph, they're perfect. Gorgeous mouth period, as a matter of fact, she thought.

At the end, they clapped and he bowed. They laughed.

"Can we go outside?" asked Taj on the verge of boredom.

"Yes, you may," said Niki who watched them leave, then turned her attention back to Kevin.

"That was so good that if I didn't already have the knives I would definitely be tempted to buy them."

"Thanks," said Kevin. "Now let me really have it."

"No, that was great. You weren't nervous. You have knowledge of the product. You answered our questions—even to the ones you weren't sure about, you gave an intelligent, honest response. I like when you took the time to look in the book to verify your response. Let's 'em know you don't mind showing that you don't know everything and that you are willing to do the work to find out. It was really good, and I wouldn't say that if it wasn't. You are ready."

"Well, I do appreciate that Sister Riley," he said.

"No problem, Brother Mitchell," said Niki.

"How did you know my last name?" he asked.

"It's on your book."

"How did you know mine?" asked Niki.

"Taj told me."

Niki got up and turned on the radio. As Kevin packed up his materials, he was singing the song on the radio, and Niki noticed his beautiful voice.

"Do you sing in a choir?" she asked.

"Not now. I did in college."

"Well, when you finally get to Way Maker Ministries and become a member—and I'm sure you will—you will also have to join the choir. You have a soloist's voice."

"Yeah, right," Kevin shrugged.

"I'm serious, and I'm a hard critic. Nobody ever told you that before?"

"I've been told. Now I know some people who can really sing and I can't touch them," he said.

His modesty was very attractive.

The phone rang. Niki went over and grabbed it up.

"I'm on my way," said Erica.

"Right on time," said Niki.

"Well, I'll check you folks later," Kevin said heading towards the door. "Have a blessed evening."

"Catch you later," Niki said.

She went outside to check to see if the kids looked presentable. When she saw Mia, she took her by the hand and went back into the apartment.

"Stay out here and tell Erica I'll be right out so she won't have to get out of the car," she yelled back at the older children.

"Look at you, Mia. We're going to have to wipe your face and brush that hair. Let me look at your clothes," she said standing back looking at her daughter, not noticing any dirt, just her shirt hanging out. "They're okay, I guess."

Niki tucked her daughter's shirt back inside her shorts, washed her face, and brushed her hair. Then they went downstairs. Taj and Maya were in Erica's car. Mia got in the backseat with them, and Niki got up front.

"Evening, Sister," she said.

"Evening to you, too. Have you been praying?" asked Erica.

"You know that's right," answered Niki.

"It's all up to you, now. God has put it out there," Erica said, making sure Niki understood that there was absolutely nothing she could do to hook her up since some folks, not necessarily Niki, were looking for that hookup. Girlfriend was on her own, and she hoped she had made that clear.

Niki said, "Girl, that is such a done deal we can move on to the next miracle. Where're we going?"

"Well, I wanted to take the kids to Laser Land. They'll love it. Or we can go to the mall. It's up to you," said Erica.

"What's Laser Land?" asked Maya.

"An amusement center with lots of fun things to do. Want to go?" Then looking at Niki, she said, "You and I can hit the mall any time."

"Okay," Niki said, as they kids all started shouting, "Please, Mommy, please."

They had a ball at Laser Land. They played laser tag, the kids drove race cars, played games, and just ran all over the place. The time flew.

"We can't keep Sister Erica out too late," Niki said as they regrouped at one of the benches. "She has to go to work in the morning. And you guys need to start going to bed at 9:30 to get back into school mode."

"One more game, please Mom…" pleaded Taj.

"What did I say?"

"Yes, ma'am," said Taj thinking, *You win some you lose some, but it was worth a try.*

They stopped and got some ice cream and Erica dropped them off. This had been a wonderful day.

CHAPTER 10

RIIINGGGG!

"Hello."

"Hey, Ma."

"Hey, baby. Jim, it's Niki. How're my babies?"

"We're fine. How are you?"

"Same old, same old, just missing my babies," said Jean.

"Dad called when I was at the store and said you were planning to come down this weekend," said Niki.

"You know he laid you out to whoever would listen for leaving his grand-babies home alone in that great big strange city that you know nothing about. He wouldn't care if you just went to the car to get something out of it and didn't drive anywhere. Pack his babies up and take them with you. He is over-protective to a fault."

"I know, Ma. I don't remember him being that overprotective with me."

"Think about it, Nik. When was he *not* there? When you were in high school, he didn't go to see the games—he went to see *you cheer*. When you didn't come home for the weekend while you were in college—he was up there to visit you. And when you joined that church—he came to spend the weekend with you to check it out. Came back and assured me that you were okay, and that it was a pretty nice church."

"I guess you're right, Ma. So where were you?"

"Your dad was not dragging me all over creation following behind you. Y'all made me tired just watching you rip, race, and run. And you could go, girl. Look how you just packed up and was out of here. You get a whim and you gone. He can try to keep up with you, but I'll be here to take care of the home front," Jean explained.

"I knew you had a logical explanation. So when will you get here?"

"I'll have to have your father call you back. A friend just stopped by and he's tangled up in conversation with him. He'll have to give you all the details. Love you, baby. Talk to you later," said Jean.

"Ma, wait. Where's Rae?" asked Niki.

"She's in jail, baby. It all caught up with her. She got to pull time now. Got her at the Women's Correctional Facility in Fulton. I had a feeling it was going to come to this," said Jean.

"Dag, dog, dag, dag, dog," Niki said frustrated and disapppointed that she couldn't save her cousin.

"Don't beat yourself up, baby. You did the best you could. For her and Sam. People have got to take responsibility for themselves. You don't have time to be worrying about no grown folks, you got my grandbabies to raise. So don't worry about it. Just pray."

Niki knew her mother was right, but she just felt so bad. Rae was her special cousin. After all the tragedy her family had gone through, she wanted to at least be able to help save one of them.

When Rae's mother Aunt Tee committed suicide, all hell had broken loose. Crime and murder in Fulton had become an epidemic. Three months after his mother's death, Rae's oldest brother Leonard was killed in a shootout that they said was drug related. Rae and her younger sister Angie went to live with their father and the stepmother they had been taught to hate. The girls were so devastated from the death of their mother and big brother that they just spun out of control. There wasn't much their father or stepmother could do with them. After years of chaotic living, Angie got pregnant by Howard, the son of a prominent elected official. Angie was madly in love with him and wanted desperately for him to rescue her from her father's house.

Howard told Angie that to spare his father any embarrassment over the pregnancy, they were going to elope. That night he took her into some woods to make love to her. After they had sex, while she laid there, he pulled out a gun and shot her seven times. Then he set her body on fire to hide the evidence. Her body was burnt beyond recognition.

Angie had just graduated from high school. Since Rae had dropped out of high school earlier, Niki's incentive for Angie to stay in school was that she promised to buy her any graduation ring she wanted. The engraving on her high school graduation ring that she was wearing when she was murdered was the only thing not destroyed by the fire. She wore her graduation gift for only two months before it became the evidence used to identify her body.

When the judge asked Howard what was the last thing she said to him before he shot her, he answered, "She told me she loved me." He didn't want to disgrace his family by bringing an illegitimate child into the world. So that's how he decided to get rid of his problem after Angie had refused to have an abortion.

That was the straw that broke the camel's back for Rae. She ran away and had been a part of the underworld ever since. Niki tried to save her, and for a while it seemed like she was getting through. But something always sucked Rae back in.

Was I ever able to help Rae? she wondered. "Oh, Lord, please be with her where she is now. Don't let the enemy snatch the Word from her. Reveal Yourself to her in a new way that she may be a true light in jail amongst all those others who so desperately need You. Empower her, Lord. Bring good out of this horrible situation for Your Kingdom, Lord. Help us all make the most of our time until You return for us. Amen."

CHAPTER 11

"Who does Rae think she is? I'll bust her up," said Queenie, gang leader of the Regals.

"I know, always acting like she's reading the Bible. If she was so religious, why she up in here?" asked Cookie, Queenie's right hand.

"She frontin'; I say we slam her one time to let her know she ain't better than nobody in here," said Queenie.

"When, Queenie? 'Cause she needs to know who run things in here," said Cookie.

"Tonight. The sooner the better,"

"The showers?"

"Yep, the showers."

That evening, as Rae was rinsing the shampoo out of her hair in the shower, eyes closed, warm water and suds flowing down her face and body, suddenly she felt an excruciating pain on the back of her head that went threw her whole entire body. Her knees got rubbery, and she could no longer hold herself up. She fell to the shower floor, and then felt her body being beaten and kicked while hearing women's voices laughing.

"You ain't better than nobody Miss Anti-social. You shouldn't have left that Bible in yo' cell, what you gonna do now?"

As Rae lay on the floor naked, being beaten and kicked, all the pain suddenly left her body. Eyes closed, she remembered the story of Shadrach, Meshach and Abednego in the fiery furnace, who were untouched by the fire or by the smoke. The fire had been so hot that the guards who were ordered to put them in the furnace got burnt up, yet when the Hebrew boys were let out of the furnace they did not even smell like smoke. Rae knew that the same God who protected them in the furnace was protecting her now, and she just laid on the shower floor and praised Him.

"Thank You, Father. I love You, Lord. Hallelujah! Glory to God!" laughed and praised Rae.

"What??!!" yelled Queenie.

"This chick is crazy!" cried Cookie.

"For real, let's get out of here; she's looney!"

Fifteen minutes later, Rae still lay on the shower floor praying, laughing and crying at the same time, water still bouncing off her naked body, when Sharia came in.

"Rae, girl, what you doing on the floor?" cried Sharia as she bent down to help her up.

"Girl, what happened? Was it that no good, sorry Queenie? Girl, I told you she think everybody need to bow down to her. She ain't no queen for real. Somebody need to slice her one time real good."

Sharia helped Rae dry off and get dressed. Rae was still praying and singing praises to the Lord. Sharia knew that Rae had a special relationship with the Lord and had always respected her for that; however, this was the first time she had seen the power of God in operation, and she was totally amazed. She could tell from looking at Rae's naked body that she had been beaten, there were even some traces of blood left that the shower water hadn't washed all away. But the amazing thing was that somehow Rae didn't appear to hurt at all! All Rae kept doing was praising the Lord and laughing when Sharia knew she, herself, would have been plotting their murder. As Sharia observed this woman who obviously was operating in a different realm even though she was still here in jail, she felt drawn to her. She wanted what Rae had on the inside of her that could cause her to act like this under these circumstances.

The next morning at breakfast, Sharia went over and sat by Rae.

"How you doin' this morning?" Sharia asked.

"I'm okay. Thanks for your help last night," said Rae

"Do you know who beat you up? I bet it was that sorry Queenie. I got a blade and I'll slice her up if she try that mess with me. You can have it if you want."

"No, thanks. It doesn't matter who it was. I'm not hurt and I'm gonna just pray for my attackers. And remember, I gotta stay out of trouble so I can get out of here. My kids need me. God will take care of whoever it was that attacked me," said Rae coolly and calmly.

"Girl, I got to have some of what you got. Everybody in here needs it. Teach me how to be like that, 'cause I'm telling you, I am ready to slice whoever did this to you, nice as you are," said Sharia.

"Forgive them, Sharia, they don't know 'cause they haven't been taught. Now I'm not a teacher but I know enough to share what I do know to help some of the women in here that want to know just like my cous' helped me. If you're serious about wanting to learn more about the things of God, come with me to the Warden's office and let's ask if I can start a Bible study. It'll be one that's different from the regular services we have, but where we can read and discuss the Bible and really get to know God. My cousin, Niki, always told me just going to church ain't gonna get it. We got to dig, and I mean deep, to get what we need out of the Word. I can help. I know I can. What do you think?" asked Rae.

"Let's go, girl, I'm with you!" exclaimed Sharia.

The warden was agreeable to let Rae start a Bible study, even offering to order new Bibles for the women who wanted to attend.

Queenie and Cookie were so astonished that there was absolutely nothing mentioned of the incident to anyone. Their curiosity about Rae got the better of them. When they heard about Rae's Bible study sessions, they were on the front row. They listened intently as Rae read from the Bible, interpreted what she had read, gave real life examples that applied to them in order to help paint an even clearer picture for those in attendance.

At the end of the first session when Rae shared about salvation, Queenie and Cookie were the first to give their lives to Christ.

CHAPTER 12

As Niki waited for her father to call back, her mind wandered to the rest of her family. When she had discovered that Sam—perfect Sam, with perfect parents, perfect upbringing, perfect job, a perfect husband—was on drugs, she vowed she would never let her own family be destroyed. Thus her mission began.

Had it not been for Aunt Katie, she surely would have gone crazy. The saying was that Jean carried Niki five months and Aunt Katie carried her four. Both of Niki's aunts adored her and she them. Aunt Tee was there nurturing her while she grew up along with her own children on an almost daily basis while Jean worked.

Aunt Katie lived in Washington, D.C., but the bond between them seemed the strongest of Grandma Laura Lee's three daughters. Jean was a strict disciplinarian and that spirit was passed on to Niki. Aunt Tee had her own children. Aunt Katie never had any children of her own, and Niki naturally fell into the position.

Niki was quite possessive of Aunt Katie. Because she lived out of town and was so loving, kind, and giving, she had several play children that looked to her like a mother. But when Niki was there, she let it be known that that was her Aunt Katie. When she called the house and someone besides Aunt Katie answered the phone, Niki asked to speak to "My Aunt Katie" like that was her first, middle, and last name.

"Katie, your niece is on the phone," they would say, knowing it was her, not by her voice but by her possessive reputation.

Niki needed her Aunt Katie to keep her sane, to keep things in perspective. They would talk for hours about anything and everything. Aunt Katie talked her through high school, college, family tragedy, boyfriends, jobs, marriage, and when Niki started talking about Jesus, Aunt Katie was the only one who would listen. Then one day Aunt Katie started talking about Jesus and all the things she was doing in the kingdom of God. Niki was thrilled. She praised God for giving her such a wonderful gift as Aunt Katie.

Niki had done everything right up to that point, but it didn't do any good. She came to the realization that all her education, activities, material possessions, perfect looking marriage, and home life could not save her family. This was around the time the *Malcolm X* movie came out. Niki concluded that she had been had, she had been took, led astray, run amuck, bamboozled and hoodwinked into believing that securing the American dream was all she had to do to live a happy and fulfilling life.

Niki began to reeducate herself, first about her people. She had been taught about Martin Luther King, Jr., and other black history, but nothing about Malcolm X. All she knew was that Martin Luther King, Jr. was the good guy, and Malcolm X was the bad guy. But she didn't understand what made him bad like she understood what made Martin good. Therefore, she read every word she could find written about Malcolm X, beginning with his autobiography. Next were the FBI files. What a contrast. She read all of his speeches, she listened to tapes and watched videos over and over until her eyes began to open. She became more and more enlightened. She entered essay contests and won prizes for the commentaries she wrote on the things she had learned.

She thought, *If I was this misinformed about my heritage, then I know I don't know squat about the Bible.* So she used the same approach and delved headfirst into the Bible. She joined the Fulton Christian Center, a Word of Faith church, a church that taught the Word of God in a way that developed faith in the hearts of the people who heard it. She spent much time in prayer developing a strong relationship with her heavenly Father. She was growing up in the things of God. That's when she began to change. She took Bible courses, attended Bible studies, and even convinced others to get up early and pray with her because she read that you should seek first the kingdom of God. It was all good, but she drove the people around her crazy. All she did was listen to teaching tapes and Christian music CDs, watch Christian TV, and read Christian books.

The first question she asked folks she met was, "Are you saved?" Of course, her family thought she had lost it. But that didn't deter her. It even took its toll on her job, for when she saw a lot of activity that wasn't on the up and up in high level management, she knew it was time to go. And right in the nick of time, because that was when Sam was heavy into drugs and it was about to threaten her home. But God knew and led her home and anointed her to stand guard so the demons couldn't come in.

She became a warrior, practicing daily warfare until it was just not in her to fight anymore. It wasn't because she gave up, but because Sam had made his choice. He chose not to fight *with* Niki, but *against* her, and a house divided against itself cannot stand. Therefore, Niki had asked for wisdom on what to do in this situation and here she was, beginning a new life in Zion.

"Hey, baby," her father finally had called her back.

"Hi, Daddy, what's up?"

"How are my grandbabies?"

"Doing good. We have met some really nice people. And Taj couldn't be better. We have two big football players who happen to be teachers, college graduates, and real good role models for him living right under us. They spend time with him so he has strong male influences in his life. I have met a really good friend, Erica, from the church. She took us out and we had a ball. This was really of God. So you can relax," said Niki.

"Not until I see for myself. Did your mother tell you that we plan to come this weekend if it's okay with you?"

"Yeah, she said you'd fill me in on the details. Can't wait to see you. What time will you get here?"

"We're leaving Friday morning. We're going to take our time, enjoy the scenery. Need anything?" asked Jim.

"Just hugs," answered Niki.

"Got plenty of them. We'll see you Friday, sweetheart."

"Okay, Daddy. Tell Ma I'll talk to her later."

"I will. Bye, baby."

"Bye, Daddy, love you."

"Love you, too, baby. See ya soon."

After breakfast on Friday, they cleaned the apartment spic and span. Niki called Erica.

"Hey, whatcha doing this weekend?"

"Just running some errands. What's up?" asked Erica.

"My parents will be in town, and I would love for you to meet them."

"I would love to meet them. When are they coming?" Erica asked.

"Friday," answered Niki.

"Maybe I can stop by after work," Erica said.

"Do that. They'll probably just want to chill Friday after that long ride so we'll be here. Just stop on by," said Niki.

"Cool. How're the kids?" asked Erica.

"Blessed. We had the best time the other day. Thanks again for that."

"Girl, I bet I had more fun than anybody," said Erica.

"You were into it, girl, that's for sure."

"I refuse to get old," Erica said.

"I hear ya," laughed Niki.

"Talk to you later."

"Bye."

Knock, knock, knock. Niki looked thru the peephole and saw her father. She swung the door open. "DADDY!" she shouted and squeezed his neck. The kids came flying out of their rooms.

"GRANDDADDY! GRANDMA!" They jumped on him and almost knocked him down. He managed to make his way to the sofa and sit down while they hugged and kissed all over him. Niki was hugging her mother. When she finished, the kids left Granddaddy and grabbed Grandma.

"My babies, my precious babies. Thank God, you are all right," cried Jean.

"Oh, Ma," said Niki.

When they all felt that they had sufficiently hugged and kissed, Niki said, "Sit down, relax, get comfortable. I'll go get your stuff out of the car."

"I'll have to help you with the suitcase, Niki," said Jim, "it's pretty heavy." He got up and together they went outside to the car.

"Let me see if Kevin and Randy are home," said Niki.

When she knocked on their door, Randy opened it.

"Hey, I want you guys to meet my parents. They came down for a visit. Is Kevin here?"

"Yep, I'll get him. We'll be right out," said Randy.

The guys came over to the car while Niki and her dad were getting the bags out.

"Daddy, this is Randy and this is Kevin. They are the best neighbors in the world and the kids love them."

"You are some big guys," Jim said.

They laughed.

"Nice to meet you, sir. Let us get those bags for you," said Kevin.

"Thanks, man," said Jim.

Randy and Kevin followed Niki and Jim up to the apartment with the suitcase and bags.

"Just put them anywhere. This is my mom, Mrs. Jean Harris," said Niki.

They greeted her and shook hands. Niki continued on about the guys as if she was introducing the evening's speakers to an audience.

"They both graduated from the same university. They played on the same championship football team, and they are school teachers. They aspire to be championship football coaches, and they are excellent role models for our children, especially our young black boys. I am pretty lucky to have them for my neighbors and friends," praised Niki.

They were blushing and grinning from ear to ear. Neither one of them could say a word. Niki wasn't just saying that to make her parents or them feel good. She really and truly believed what she said.

"Well, since my daughter speaks so highly of you, you must be all right," said Jean.

"Nice to meet you," said Randy.

"Nice to meet you, ma'am," Kevin said, looking shy again.

Niki concluded that if Kevin didn't know you, he went into some type of shell. But after he got to know you, you couldn't shut him up.

"Hope to see you again before you leave," said Randy as they walked towards the door.

"Thanks for the help," said Jim.

And they were gone.

"They seem like nice fellas," said Jean.

"The best," said Niki.

"Do you like them, Maya?" asked Jim.

"Hum, huh. They're real cool," she said.

"They're real nice, Granddaddy, especially Kevin. He buys me bubble gum," said Mia.

"They said they are going to teach me all about football and show me some cool moves, Granddaddy," said Taj.

"All right then," said Jim. Then leaning into Niki's ear he said, "Still, you watch them."

"Don't worry, Dad. You ain't raised no fool," said Niki.

"That's my girl. Where's the bathroom?"

"I'll give you a tour, Granddaddy," said Taj.

As they made themselves at home, Niki checked on the meal she had cooked. She prayed that it tasted as good as it looked.

"Are you guys ready for something to eat?"

"You cooked? You mean we don't have to take you out to eat?" asked Jim.

"Tomorrow you do, but not tonight. Aren't I thoughtful?" responded Niki, laughing.

"Yeah. I could use a bite to eat. Not too much now, I'm cutting back," said Jim.

"I'll fix his plate, Niki. I know what 'cutting back' means," said Jean.

"Okay, Ma. I'll fix the kids' plates."

While they were eating, there was a knock on the door. It was Erica. Niki made the introductions.

"Get a plate," she instructed Erica.

"Okay. Your daughter sure can cook, Mrs. Harris. She has been feeding me ever since I met her."

"Sowing food as seed into others to make sure my kids always eat," said Niki.

Everyone thoroughly enjoyed the meal. The kids crashed all over their granddaddy in front of the TV.

"I'm going to unpack some things, Niki. Nice meeting you, Erica," said Jean.

"Wonderful meeting you, Mrs. Harris, and you, too, Mr. Harris," she said, walking towards the living room. "Will you be coming to church during your visit?"

"Don't know yet," said Jim, basking in the love that was being poured on him.

"Well, enjoy your visit. I'm gonna go on home, Nik. Got some work to do," said Erica.

"Okay. I'll talk to you later," she said.

"These people sure do appear to be nice, but you keep your antennas up. Can't be too careful where my babies are concerned," said Jean after Erica left.

"I know, Ma."

The next morning they went out for breakfast. Niki drove them past the church and downtown. It was a beautiful day and very crowded downtown. There was some festival event in the park going on, and people were everywhere. Jim and Jean didn't want to get out of the car.

"We don't do crowds. There's too much happening around here. Let's go to a nice, quiet mall," said Jean.

So to the mall they went. They bought the kids school clothes and supplies.

"This is a big help, Ma and Dad. Thanks."

"You're welcome, baby. Anything for our grandbabies," said Jean.

They had already walked breakfast off and were ready to eat again. Actually Jim was ready to go home, so they stopped and picked up something to eat.

When they arrived home with the food, Jean and Niki set up the table so that everyone could serve themselves.

"We go to 9:00 a.m. church service, but we can go earlier at 7:00 or later at 11:00. Which one do you want to go to?" Niki asked her mother while setting the table.

"I'll let you know," Jean said.

Niki knew what that meant. They weren't going to either service. Oh, well, at least she had learned not to push.

The next morning Niki let them sleep in, got the kids up and went to church. Her parents were up having coffee when they got back.

"How was church?" asked Jean.

"Great as usual," answered Niki. And she left it at that.

Jean cooked Sunday dinner.

"Hmmm hm!" said Taj. "You still got it, Grandma."

"Thank you, my precious darling heart," Jean said, grinning at her pride and joy. Not another grandparent could love a grandson like Jean loved Taj. Except Jim. They adored the girls just as much, but that boy was just special because he was their only boy.

The week went by pretty fast. They rode around Zion sightseeing. Niki took them to see Tina. It was good seeing her again. By Wednesday, they had become bored.

"Niki, I think we're going to head on out early in the morning so we can get back home before it gets dark," said Jim.

"Dad, you just got here."

"Your mother and I feel much better now that we see you're doing just fine. We're really proud of you, baby."

"Thanks, Dad."

She couldn't think of anything to say to convince them to stay longer.

"Well, get a good night's sleep so you can be well rested for your drive. You know Ma isn't going to help you drive one mile." They both laughed, knowing it was true.

"That's your mother, thinking she's got a chauffeur."

"Can't keep you people out of Fulton for any length of time, like something is going on there you might miss."

"It is. Fulton is a happening town," said Jim.

"Yeah, right," she laughed.

Jim and his bride were on the rode before rush hour hit the next morning. It was smooth sailing all the way.

"I'm sure proud of our daughter. She makes up her mind to do something, and she just does it and doesn't look back," said Jim.

"She's made from good stock," said Jean.

"God take care of our babies. Preserve them until the day of Your return," prayed Jim.

CHAPTER 13

"Way Maker Ministries. This is Tonya. How may I direct your call?" said a sweet, pleasant anointed voice that made you smile.

"May I speak to Sister Erica Scott, please?" responded Niki.

"Just one moment, please."

"Personnel, this is Sister Erica Scott, how may I help you?"

"Hi, Sis. I know you're busy."

"Hey, girl. Always busy. How's everybody? How's mom and dad?"

"Gone. Left this morning. The older you get, the more you hate to leave home, I guess. They couldn't make it a week without thinking they were missing something back home. But we really enjoyed the time we did have with them."

"Did they make it to church?" asked Erica.

"No, and I didn't make them feel bad about it either. I'm growing."

"Good for you."

"I started my classes. And God is so good. They are in the middle of make-up classes, and I can make up the ones I missed and might even be able to graduate the next go round," said Niki, thrilled about the possibility.

"Girl, that's God," said Erica.

"I will be up there today to listen to a couple of classes on tape and get them done," said Niki.

"You are rolling," said Erica.

"I see my job is still posted. What's the status?" asked Niki.

"It will probably close by the end of the week. Then I'll give all the qualified apps to the Controller on Monday. Once he decides who he wants to interview, we'll set it up and give you a call."

"Sounds groovy. Well I'm going to get the kids straight, then I'll be on up there. Probably won't see you, so I'll catch you later."

"Okay. Kiss the kids for me."

Niki went up to the New Members office. People were everywhere listening to tapes, trying to make up classes so they could graduate and become active. She had thoroughly enjoyed her "live" class last Thursday. She got her course book and schedule of classes. She was impressed with the teacher, Brother Thomas. He had an anointing to preach and reminded her of Pastor. Clearly the same spirit was on the people she had heard from the pulpit.

She also enjoyed the video of the classes held for those who couldn't attend the live classes for whatever reason. Now with the make-up classes on cassette tape, surely she could finish up in time to graduate, especially since she wasn't working yet. *They are most accommodating. Erica said it took some people two and three years to finish all their classes. Why would it take someone that long with all these ways and means by which to get it done?Nothing to it but to do it. Just lazy procrastination. There you go judging again. Chill, Nik. Please forgive me, Father.*

School started for the kids. Niki drove them to the bus stop and waited with them until the bus came. Then she went to church and took a class. She was home waiting for them when they arrived back from school. This schedule continued until she completed all of her classes. Niki learned so much in those classes that she was more fired up than ever before. At the end of her last class, she was so elated she could hardly stand it. She passed her test with flying colors and was ready to graduate.

She smiled for her graduation picture harder than she had for any other graduation picture she had ever taken. She was almost there. All Pastor had to do was impart the vision into her at graduation and it would be on then.

She invited Kevin and Randy to her graduation. She had to be there early to join over 300 graduates to line up and get their instructions. It was just like school. Randy couldn't make it, but Kevin did and brought the kids with him. Niki heard them clapping for her when they called her name to receive her certificate. It was a special moment in her life.

After the ceremony, the graduates were instructed to go over to the fellowship hall. She met Kevin and the kids outside.

"I have to go to the reception now."

"I'll take the kids on home with me then. Just stop by when you finish up here," Kevin said.

Niki gave him a big hug. "You're a sweetheart. Thanks," she said. She hugged and kissed each child and told them she would see them shortly.

She went over to the fellowship hall where all the graduates gathered in order to be recruited by the different ministries. She was further overwhelmed. There were so many to choose from. She saw Children's Ministry, Nursing Home Ministry, Parking Ministry, Athletic Ministry, Dance, Substance Abuse, Singles and Marriage Ministries. You name it, she saw it. Something for everyone. She got refreshments and wandered around in almost a daze.

This is an awesome church, and I'm a part of it. I don't know what to choose.

64

They were calling out to her, "Over here."

They had candy, pens, and pads as incentives. There were flyers and all kinds of things to make their ministries look like the best one to join. Niki couldn't think straight. All she could do was thank God that now she was an official part of such a great work. And she intended to do her part to the best of her ability. Therefore, God would have to place her in the ministry where He wanted her to serve.

She took handouts from most of the ministries to read later. The entire graduation experience was almost as overwhelming as the first time she was in the sanctuary when she couldn't stop crying. She felt tears of joy coming up now and decided to leave so that she could let them flow freely. She ran to her car and praised God all the way home.

CHAPTER 14

Now that the kids were in school and she had graduated from New Members classes, and her paperwork was submitted for the only job she ever truly wanted, she had to do the hardest thing in the world for her to do—wait! This became quite a challenge for her because she never could keep still. Niki was a producer. She had to always be involved with something productive. That is how her business got started. She hadn't left her job in order to start her own business back in Fulton. But after being home day in and day out, her creative juices began to flow, and her own business was born. Everybody—kids and adults alike—wore her original custom designed shirts and caps. It was really a hobby that she didn't pick back up when she moved. She didn't feel like picking it back up now either. She wanted to work at the church.

She didn't want to be a pest so she only called Erica every other day.

"Hey, Erica. Any word on my job?"

"I'm waiting on the Controller to tell me who he wants to interview. I'll let you know once things are all set."

"Okay. Talk to you later," said a solemn Niki.

She had been thriving off of all the excitement. Now that things were quieting down, she was going through thrill withdrawals.

Brother Vincent Coles was the Controller, graduate of Princeton, brain to the bone, from up north, so these southerners took some getting use to. He was perfect for his position being a straight-laced, unshakable, immovable, uncompromising, perfectionist with a zero tolerance for error. It was all good until you got to the zero tolerance for error since nobody, except Jesus, was perfect. However, he was a firm believer that this ministry was built on excellence, and he accepted nothing less than perfection.

"Brother Vincent, have you made a decision on those outreach accountant applications?" asked Erica.

"I have, but I was waiting to see if I heard anything else from God," Vincent responded.

"We want to get all of the outreach positions filled by the end of the month. That means the sooner I can get your choices, the sooner I can set up the interviews. How much longer do you need?" asked Erica.

"I'll bring them to you today," said Vincent.

"Thank you. Are you free to interview on the days listed on the schedule attached to the apps?" asked Erica.

"Yes, those times are fine with me," said Vincent.

"I'll set up the interviews and forward you a schedule with the names when I receive your choices," said Erica.

"That will be fine. Thank you, Sister Erica. I apologize for the delay. But this person has to be called here. This is a very important position. I was just making sure."

"I understand, Brother Vincent."

When Erica received the choice applications from Vincent she noticed that Niki's was on the top.

That's a good sign, she thought. She called Niki right away.

"This is Sister Erica Scott from Way Maker Ministries, Personnel Department. May I please speak with Sister Nicole Riley?"

"Girl, what?" responded Niki excited to hear the official tone in Erica's voice.

Erica laughed at Niki's impatience, comfortable with the fact that she was a competent professional who was real enough to be herself.

"Can you come in for an interview Monday at 10:00?" asked Erica.

"Yes, I can. Are there any special instructions?" Niki asked, sounding professional like Erica.

"Yes. When you come into the lobby, go to the receptionist's desk and let her know that you are here to interview for the outreach accountant position. She will instruct you from there."

"Do I need to bring anything?"

"You can bring a calculator because you will be given a test."

"What! You are the testingest people I have ever seen or heard of," Niki said, all professionalism gone.

They both laughed.

"You'll be fine, girl," said Erica.

"What kind of test?" asked Niki.

"An accounting test. The Controller is a Princeton graduate and a stickler for that kind of thing. You can handle that, right, cause I can't..."

Niki cut her off.

"I told you I got this."

"Handle your business then. I'll talk to you later. Got to set up more interviews," said Erica.

"What does my competition look like?" she asked.

"Bye, Niki," said Erica.

"Just testing. See, you're rubbing off on me already."

Niki was at the church at 9:30 a.m. She let the receptionist know that she was the outreach accountant coming to claim her job. The receptionist was amused and smiled at Niki, instructing her to have a seat in the lobby. She called Vincent to inform him that Niki was here for her interview. Vincent was nowhere near ready, and Niki would have to wait. She was early anyway.

As Niki waited patiently, she observed the daily operations of the ministry. She saw all kinds of workers, maintenance people, cooks, engineers, media people, and bookstore staff. She saw independent contractors, children from the daycare, and delivery trucks of all kinds. She saw musicians carrying keyboards and bass guitars. This was a busy place, a major operation. She almost forgot for a minute that it was a church. It looked so much like a business. Well, it was.

Then there were the people sitting in the lobby waiting with her, who were there for counseling. There were married couples and the poor in need of assistance. There she was overwhelmed again. But she had to maintain her composure this time because she was on a mission today. *Focus, focus, focus.* She began to pray in tongues until she calmed down. That peace that only the Holy Ghost can give works every time.

A man came up to her.

"Sister Nicole Riley?" he asked.

Niki stood up.

"Yes."

The man extended his hand.

"Hello, I'm Brother Vincent Coles, Controller here at Way Maker Ministries."

"Nice to meet you," Niki said, firmly shaking his hand.

Vincent liked that. One point for Niki.

"Did Sister Erica inform you of the test you will be taking?" asked Vincent.

"Yes, she did," answered Niki.

"We'll have you take the test first, then I'll meet with you for the interview. Please follow me."

He directed Niki to a conference room.

"Take all the time you need. Use that phone to dial Extension 367 when you are finished. Do you have a calculator?"

"Yes, I do."

"This is not the CPA exam, so feel free to use it. Here is scratch paper and plenty of pencils. Do you have any questions?"

"No."

"Okay, you can get started," Vincent said and left.

Niki read over the test. *Wow, this is serious. You almost have to have a degree in accounting to pass this test. At least have taken college accounting courses,* Niki thought. *This is great. This test will help eliminate my competition. Let's go, Lord!*

The test took Niki back to college, Mr. Hutt's principles of accounting class. She knocked it out, checked it twice, and dialed Extension 367.

"This is Nicole Riley. I have completed my accounting test."

"I'll be right there."

Vincent checked her answers right there and Niki got one wrong. She was devastated.

"Why did you select that answer?" he asked.

Niki's explanation was logical and well thought out, and Vincent could see how Niki would have selected that answer coming from a profit-oriented environment.

"We have to be mindful of the differences in accounting for a profit versus a non-profit entity such as a church," said Vincent.

"I understand," said Niki, feeling a lot better that she had not completely blown the question.

"You have a very impressive resumé, Sister Nicole. But we wouldn't have called you here if it wasn't. So why should we hire you?" he asked coming straight to the point.

At that precise moment, an anointing came upon Niki, and it was no longer her, but the greater One that lived on the inside of her that spoke.

Niki yielded, "Because in my 15 years of experience I have probably seen most types of accounting transactions. I have worked in every area of accounting, from auditing to internal controls, to daily operations, to financial reporting. I have worked in the public, private, government, and non-profit arenas. I volunteered at my church in Virginia and helped to establish several ministries including a drug rehabilitation ministry and a Christian radio station. With my knowledge of accounting, experiences, and the help of the Holy Ghost, nothing is going to happen in outreach accounting that I won't be able to handle, Brother Vincent."

He sat back in his seat visibly impressed. For some reason he believed her. He thought about the rest of the interview questions. What Niki said just about covered all of them. *Time to switch gears. Later for the format. I'll ask her the situation type questions at the end of the interview. But for now let's talk,* Vincent thought.

"We are currently reorganizing to separate the outreach part of the ministry from the local church administratively. Outreach will have its own administrative staff. Should you be the chosen candidate, you will be the outreach accountant over all of the outreach finances reporting to me."

As he went on to explain the future plans of the ministry, Niki listened intently. When Vincent finished, he asked, "Do you have any questions?"

"Is there any travel involved?" asked Niki.

"Yes, the outreach accountant will be the overseer of the engagement finances on the road. Therefore, you will be required to travel with the engagement team."

Niki thought, *God will have to work that part of the job out.*

Finally Vincent said, "I have to ask you the rest of these questions for the record."

Niki took that to mean, "You have passed this test, now we have to do the formal thing."

They went through the list, Vincent asking, Niki answering, and Vincent recording her responses. After the last formalities were taken care of, Vincent stood up and said, "Well, it has certainly been a pleasure talking to you today."

"The pleasure was all mine," said Niki.

They shook hands, and she thanked him for the interview. She also let him know that she was looking forward to hearing from him soon.

Vincent escorted her to the door.

She went to her car and praised God all the way home.

CHAPTER 15

Niki did not like waiting. She began looking at the soaps again. Duke and Tara were back on Central Hospital, and now they had a son. Whoever cast that boy should get a bonus. He's perfect.

Niki had really been into Duke and Tara since college. She remembered one day after she graduated and was working downtown, leaving a very important meeting to go see their wedding at The Gas and Electric Company where a crowd had gathered for the same reason.

She had had it bad right before she got saved. She taped all the channel seven soaps that came on between 1:00 and 4:00 p.m. each and every day. When she came home, she changed clothes, cooked dinner, fixed her family's plates, and ate her dinner watching all the soaps she had taped. She had it down pat. This was her weekday routine.

Then one day during an electrical storm, lightening fried the VCR, and she could no longer record her soaps. Instead of going out immediately and buying another VCR, she was relieved in a way. Said she was going to see how long she could go without seeing the soaps. Subconsciously, she knew she was addicted, but nobody was getting hurt, and she was taking care of home and work, so what the heck. She felt like maybe her husband felt the same way about drugs—nobody was getting hurt, and he was taking care of home and work. But Niki did something about her addiction. She took the opportunity to break the habit and didn't go back to the soaps even after they eventually got another VCR. Oh, she watched when Duke and Tara first returned to Central Hospital after ten years. Who didn't? However, she was careful not to get hooked again, constantly telling herself how stupid and unrealistic they were. She did great, considering she was home all day.

The key was to stay busy, hence the birth of her business. She handpainted designs on sportswear. She also had caps and tote bags that displayed the Scriptures. Business was good, considering everything she sold was designed by hand. It was therapy for her, a vehicle to keep her mind at peace and at the same time allow her creative juices to flow. She did that up until she saw the green light to move to Zion. She hadn't done it since because it was for such a time as that, not this. God had something else planned for such a time as this.

She had never been more ready for anything in her life. She was anxious, which was a "no no." She knew the Bible says, "Be anxious for nothing, but in everything by prayer and supplication let your requests be made known unto God." He was going to give her the desires of her heart in His perfect timing. So what was she anxious about? She needed to relax because nothing was going to happen until she did. She forced herself not to call Erica. One day she couldn't wait any longer. She decided she would call her after she brought in the mail. There was a letter from Rae in the mail.

Dear Cous,
I got your address from Aunt Jean. She told me that she told you I was in jail, and you beat yourself up for not being able to save me. Cous, I messed up, not you. But I have forgiven myself, for I know my Father which is in heaven, who smiles down on me and is taking care of my children has forgiven me. I ask that you forgive me, too. I want to let you know that I appreciate everything you have done for me and the kids over the years. You were there for me Cous, and God is going to bless you for that. Remember, you sow a seed, you reap a harvest. You have sown many seeds into our lives. My prayer is that God grants you everything you desire more than you could ever imagine. This place is a difficult place. But Cous, I got my Bible and I got your words ringing in my ears and the Holy Spirit living in my heart. And now you won't believe it, Cous— I'm teaching a Bible study! So what you shared with me is being passed on to others. Cous, I am writing to let you know that I live to declare the works of the Lord until His return. Here's my address. Please write me soon.
Love, Rae

Tears met underneath Niki's chin by the time she finished reading the letter. She loved her cousin so much. She didn't want anything bad to happen to her, either. She felt so helpless, but then she remembered the power of prayer and Rae was in agreement, so it would work now.

Niki immediately began writing Rae back. They wrote each other at least weekly. Niki was always sending her stuff to keep her encouraged, motivated, and pumped up. Rae had been sentenced to serve five years in the Women's Correctional Facility. She was going to be on her best behavior to cut that time.

Some of Rae's letters just blew Niki's mind because Rae was becoming so intelligent, articulate, and deeply spiritual. Her penmanship was like a fancy font typewriter, unlike Niki's which was barely legible. Niki typed all her letters since she couldn't read her own writing half the time, and she didn't expect anybody else to. So she typed a letter to Rae rejoicing with her about her new calling in the midst of prison and totally forgot about calling Erica.

Still no word from Way Maker Ministries. Niki needed to be producing. Needed to bring home some bacon. She called Accountants R Us, a temporary agency that only placed professional accountants. She had worked with them in Fulton at times like these when she thought she would go stir crazy in the house. She couldn't leave the house, the church might call. And too, every time she left home she spent money, and she couldn't do that until the funds began to flow again. After all, Sam was still on drugs so child support was not a very stable means of support, and she needed to stabilize.

She called Accountants R Us and asked if they had received her paperwork that was forwarded from the Fulton office. They had, and asked her to come in to meet her Zion connections and to complete some paperwork. She made an appointment and went in. It felt good to dress up, corporate style again. It had been a while. She met with several of the placement executives, and they all assured her that based on her education and experience that she would have no problem whatsoever landing a lucrative position in Zion. Just let them know when she was ready. She asked them to hold off on aggressively trying to place her because she was working on something on her end, but by all means keep her informed of opportunities. Niki loved options. She always had at least a plan A and B. Most of the time a plan C. Like if Zion didn't fit, then the option was Bethel, North Carolina. She just had to stay away from Fulton.

The next day, Way Maker Ministries didn't call, but Accountants R Us did with a $20 per hour indefinite temporary assignment.

"Where is it located?" asked Niki.

"At a large company downtown. We cannot divulge the name of the company unless you are interested in interviewing for the position," said Cindy, a placement executive Niki had met the day before.

"That was really quick, Cindy," Niki said stalling.

"Actually I was already recruiting for the job. I was just waiting for the right person. I told the client all about you, and they are very interested in talking with you."

Niki was listening and praying at the same time. She heard from within, *That is not what I called you here to do.*

"I'm really not ready to go to work right this minute since I just got here and I'm still learning my way around," said Niki.

"I understand. It has to be tough settling in and making sure everything is taken care of. I'll keep you posted."

"Thanks for understanding, Cindy."

They hung up. *I bind you, Satan. That was a trick of the devil trying to get me off focus of what I came here to do. Thank you, Lord. Us Christians sure don't have the same problems the world has. If I told somebody of the world that the devil was trying to get me off track by offering my unemployed self $20 per hour, they would look at me like I was crazy. 'Get me off track,' some of them would say. Lord, I guess we are peculiar people.*

Niki and the kids were putting big faith pressure on the job and sowing big faith seeds and naming the seed outreach accountant position. She had learned long ago to get your children involved in what you are believing God for, because their faith and prayers are not hindered by some of the stuff that might hinder ours.

When Pastor asked for a special sacrificial offering for the construction project, Niki asked Taj what was the biggest amount they should give.

"$1,000," he said.

"Okay," said Niki.

She wrote the $1,000 check, although she was still an unemployed mother of three, and wrote on the back of the envelope, "This seed is for the outreach accountant position harvest, in Jesus' Name."

A few days later, a different executive from Accountants R Us called Niki who was just about ready to cave in, give up, and quit waiting. He had a job for Niki ten minutes away from where she lived with an annual starting salary of $47,500.

"Can I call you right back?" Niki asked.

She called the church.

"Erica, they are tempting me. I can't keep turning down these jobs when I don't know what y'all are going to do. Now I got to call this guy back today. If I'm not absolutely sure that I got the job at the church, then I'm taking this job."

"Let me call you back," said Erica.

Niki paced her apartment for 30 minutes.

"Brother Vincent, have you made your decision on the outreach accountant position?" asked Erica.

"I'm leaning towards Nicole Riley. I haven't finalized my decision and gotten back to you due to the fact that the person will not be able to start until the reconstruction of the accounting offices are complete, which will probably take a few more weeks," said Vincent.

"I just got a call from her and she is this close to accepting another position only because she is not sure if she will be selected as the outreach accountant," informed Erica.

"Oh, I see. Well then, she is definitely my choice. If she accepts, we'll inform her that it will be a few weeks before she can start due to the reconstruction," said Vincent.

"I will let her know," said Erica.

Next Erica called Pastor.

"Pastor, Brother Vincent has selected Nicole Riley for the outreach accountant position. All of her paperwork and credentials check out. Of all the candidates, she is the most qualified. We are ready to make her an offer. What salary have you selected?"

"Make her the offer of $25,000 a year," said Pastor.

"Yes, sir," said Erica wondering if she would be working with Niki or not.

One half hour after Erica had last talked to Niki, she called back.

"I would like to offer you the position of outreach accountant for an annual salary of $25,000," said Erica.

"I accept," said Niki, not hearing the salary at all. "Now let me call Accountants R Us back and turn them down."

CHAPTER 16

Now that the offer was made and accepted, Niki still found it difficult to sit around and wait for the completion of the accounting offices. She called Erica.

"Girl, I need something to do. Do you have any volunteer work I can do?"

"Always. Come in tomorrow morning."

When Niki arrived at the offices, she was introduced to Sister Karlyn. Sister Karlyn was Niki in about ten years—a strong, powerful, demon-stomping prayer warrior. She headed up the phone counseling ministry. She talked to Niki for a while.

"I was out there. Did everything I was big and bad enough to do, then the Lord got His hands on me and hasn't turned me loose from that day to this," she said in a loud, strong voice.

They had kindred spirits. Niki felt like Sister Karlyn could be her spiritual mother. Ever since she got for real saved she wanted a mother who would talk to her about Jesus. Niki loved Jean, but Niki got on Jean's nerves talking about Jesus, and Jean let Niki know it. When Niki would just call on the name of Jesus for no apparent reason, no matter who was around or who was listening, Jean would say, "Girl, you are going to worry that man to death." "What man?" Niki would ask. "Jesus," answered Jean. Niki didn't know if she was for real or not. She said it like she was for real. *Doesn't she know Jesus wants us to call on Him all the time?* Sister Karlyn sure knew it.

"So what do I do?" asked Niki.

"Listen to the caller's situation and give them the Word, relevant Scripture pertaining to their issue," explained Sister Karlyn.

"Okay. Are you going to sit with me?" asked Niki.

"No, I have my own phone to man. You have the Holy Ghost with you," said Sister Karlyn.

Niki looked nervous.

"Sister Erica said you had experience counseling people where you're from. Same thing. Erica would not have sent you to me if she didn't think you could handle it. Look, I'm going to lay hands on you and pray and you will be okay." She laid hands on Niki and prayed, "Father, in the name of Jesus, I thank you for my sister here. Anoint her with Your burden removing, yoke destroying power. She has the mind of Christ and the peace of God that passes all understanding. She has the wisdom of God to minister the Word to the callers and remove their burdens and destroy their yokes. Satan, we remind you that you are a whipped up defeated foe, and we quench every fiery dart that you have aimed this way. You are bound, and the gates of hell shall not prevail against the church. Thank you, Father, and it is in Jesus' Name that we pray. Amen. Now read your Bible until the phone rings. God will probably have you reading the exact Scripture you need to minister from at that time."

"Okay," said Niki, feeling a lot better after the prayer.

Niki was reading her Bible when the phone rang.

"This is Sister Niki. How may I help you today?"

A woman was crying on the other end of the phone. She explained that she was having marital challenges that Niki could relate to all too well. She gave her all the Scriptures she had stood on that she knew by heart. She didn't look at the Bible the whole conversation. The woman was soft spoken and Niki was speaking softly too.

Sister Karlyn yelled, "Speak up!"

Niki jumped and raised her voice slightly. She was able to stabilize the caller and get her focused on the Word. It sounded like the woman felt better. Niki felt good when she hung up. *I can do this.*

Sister Karlyn came over and said, "Look, that might have been an easy call, but demons call here, too, and you are not going to be able to soft talk them. You will have to take authority over those demons in the name of Jesus."

"Yes, ma'am," said Niki.

"Just be ready," Sister Karlyn said as she walked back to her desk.

Her phone rang and Niki listened to Sister Karlyn. She was ministering to a man.

"You got to be a man, listen to you whining. Talk like a man. Act like a man. Your wife wants a man," Sister Karlyn ministered.

Niki thought, *That's terrible. Obviously the man was hurting.*

When she hung up, Sister Karlyn sensing Niki's concerns came over and said, "We ain't got time to play with them, stroke them, or have a pity party with them. Give them the Word and move on. Then it's up to them, understand?"

Niki just nodded. Her phone rang.

"This is Sister Niki. How may I help you today?"

"Your Pastor is a demon from hell," said the caller.

"No, he ain't," Niki said before she knew it, and the caller hung up. She had messed up bad.

"What was that?" asked Sister Karlyn.

Niki was shook up.

"He said Pastor was a demon from hell and hung up on me," Niki said like a scared child.

"That's normal. You're okay. It's all right," Sister Karlyn said soothingly.

Niki was clearly shaken, but she knew she couldn't let that caller get to her. Her phone rang. *Take a deep breath.*

"This is Sister Niki. How may I help you today?"

"Look, Sister Niki," said the caller. "I tithed before and I sow seed, right? I'm an honest, hard working businessman. So why are all these bad things happening to me?"

"Like what, Brother?" she asked.

"Repo man got my car, and my credit's all messed up. I fell on some hard times and had to move back in with my parents, and they giving me the blues. My dad looks at me like I'm less than a man, and I can't stand being there, but I don't have anywhere else to go," the caller explained.

"Have you prayed about your situation, Brother?" she asked.

"Louder," yelled Sister Karlyn.

"Yes, I've prayed," said the caller.

"Would you like for me to stand in agreement with you and pray the Word over your situation?" asked Niki.

"Look, I said I have prayed. I need a breakthrough," said the caller.

"And if you keep standing and believing God for it you will have it, Brother. The Bible says you will reap if you faint not," said Niki.

"I need it like yesterday. What is God waiting for?" the man asked.

"Maybe for you to relax and trust Him," Niki said.

"You are a big help. Thanks a lot." And he hung the phone up on her.

She didn't like this. She listened to some of the other counselors and they were not having the challenges she was having. Why couldn't she get some easy calls?

"I'll try this again tomorrow, but if it doesn't get any better, this might not be my call," she told Sister Karlyn.

That night she called Erica.

"Girl, find me something else to do. I'm not called to help those people."

"What are you talking about? You told me about all those people you tried to preach to back home and now you have an audience—your callers," said Erica.

"It's not the same," said Niki.

"We're a big ministry and bigger demons are assigned to attack us. So it's just time for you to graduate to handle the big demons. You stomp on the little demons with no problem. Time to move up to the next level of glory," said Erica.

"Yeah, you're probably right," Niki said.

She was still despondent though. *Maybe tomorrow will be better.*

The next day was better. Niki had been able to effectively minister to two callers without getting hung up on when Erica called and said they needed help in distribution. Niki was glad to go stuff envelopes. That was ministry, too. As long as she was doing the Lord's work affecting people, she didn't care what it was.

Distribution was a different atmosphere altogether. The people were cool, but they checked her out. Brother Pete, the supervisor—a precious, godly man—trained her. Steve and Jamal, two distribution workers, decided to pick on her to test her sense of humor. She liked that because she could handle herself.

"Sister Niki, on your first day it is a requirement that you buy us lunch," Jamal informed her.

"Well, this is my second day," Niki said.

"Not in distribution. The lunch rule still applies," added Steve.

"Is that right? You're on staff, right? That means you get a paycheck, right? I volunteer, right? You're men, right? I'm a woman, right? Y'all got kids?" she asked.

They shook their heads no.

"Well, I got three to feed and y'all expect me to feed y'all, too? I just want to know how it works," said Niki, who had them going by now.

They ended up buying her lunch.

Music was playing, some workers were listening to the Word. She liked it better in distribution. She asked to stay there.

She saw Sister Karlyn at church.

"You kicked me to the curb, but that's okay," she said.

"They needed me in distribution, Sister Karlyn," said Niki.

"Praise the Lord. That's all right. May the Lord be with you as you stuff envelopes," said Sister Karlyn.

They both laughed.

The guys were fun to work with. Jamal, a Christian rapper, said he couldn't find anyone with a turntable, and he needed to record some music off of an old album. All he could find were CD players and cassette tape decks.

"I have a turntable," Niki said.

"Dag, you must be old," Jamal said, laughing.

"Look, you want to use it or not?" she said.

"Yes, yes, please," he said.

"Well chill on the age jokes. I'll give you my address. You can finally meet the kids," said Niki.

"I can't wait, as much as you talk about them. They better be all that, too," he said.

"You'll see," Niki said, just like the proud parent she was.

Taj, Maya, and Mia fell in love with Jamal, and he fell in love with them.

Jamal spent time with them rapping, doing gymnastics, karate, and teaching them just how cool it was to be a Christian.

Even though Niki loved working in distribution, during a phone conversation with Erica, she said, "Girl, you know you're wasting my skills."

The Promotions Director called Erica for a volunteer to help with some filing.

"I have the perfect volunteer, and she has some computer skills, too," Erica told Sister Linda, the Promotions Director.

"I'm out, guys," Niki told her distribution frat brothers when she found out that she had been reassigned.

"No, stay," said Steve.

"Duty calls. Got to go. Gonna miss you," she said.

"After we pledged you and everything, now you just gonna dump us," said Jamal.

"It ain't my fault. I love you though. See ya," said Niki.

In the promotions department, Niki filed. She sat in the back next to Brother Chris, the graphic artist. She saw a picture of his kids. They started talking about the pictures, then everything else. He appreciated her feedback on his projects. They discovered that they both loved Chinese food and went for the buffet right down the street from the church.

After all the filing was done, Sister Linda told Niki, "I hear you have computer skills. I'm going to have you work on promo ads."

Niki loved working on the ads. Sister Linda liked her work. Right when she was about to give her another project, Brother Vincent walked in.

"Hello, Sister Nicole."

"Hello, Brother Vincent."

"I'm glad to see you are bearing with us by volunteering your services."

Niki just nodded, waiting to hear the reason for his visit.

"We were waiting to complete the reconstruction of the offices before you started. Since they are 95% complete, how's Monday for a start date?"

"Perfect," said Niki smiling from ear to ear.

"Then I'll see you Monday at 8:00 a.m.," said Vincent.

"Thank you," said Niki.

"My harvest has come," she shouted after he had left.

CHAPTER 17

Niki was at work at 7:30 a.m. so she had to sit in the lobby until somebody came and got her. Her mind started wondering, *Why do people try to impress by showing up real early and the person they are trying to impress shows up on time or late because they aren't trying to impress the person who is waiting for them? They probably never even knew the person showed up early. Unless the new person is tacky enough to inform them, "Hey, you know I been waiting here for you for a half hour." Shut up, girl, you tripping.* Niki entertained herself with similar thoughts while she waited.

Erica showed up right at eight o'clock and came and got Niki.

"Good morning, Sister Nicole. How are you this fine day?" she asked, super excited.

"Sister Erica, I am so happy to be here this morning. What a glorious day the Lord has made in which we can rejoice and be glad," Niki said, just as excited as her friend.

They both burst out laughing at their dramatically deep professionalism.

"For real, girl. Let's go to my office. I have some forms for you to complete."

As they walked to Erica's office, she asked Niki, "Are you excited on this, your first day as a Way Maker Ministries employee?" she asked.

"Ain't He all right? I said, ain't He all right?" sang Niki.

"He's awesome, awesome," answered Erica.

"Hallelujah!" said Niki, excitement bubbling up.

In Erica's office, her radio was on down low, but Niki heard "Victory," one of her favorite songs, when it came on.

She sang, "I've got the VIC-TOR-Y through the blood of the Lamb, and my Father is God, He's the Great I Am."

The spirit hit Niki, and she jumped up and began to dance right there, in the personnel director's office, the first day on her new miracle harvest job, all dressed up.

Erica just looked at her at first. Then she laughed and before she knew it, she was up getting her praise on herself. They danced until the record was over. Then, worn out, they fell in their seats and began to pull themselves back together.

81

"Lord, how am I going to work?" asked Niki.

"Girl, you just got to pray," said Erica.

"I can do that."

Niki completed all the required paperwork. Erica gave her the grand tour, introducing her to the staff. She met the engagement staff, the media people, the day care workers, the production and music staff, the data systems people, and the ones working in the front office, and, of course, the outreach administrator. She was reintroduced to the promotions and distribution staff and the phone counselors. Last stop: the accounting department.

"I will leave you in the capable hands of your supervisor," said Erica.

They shook hands and she left.

Vincent asked if she had any questions at this point.

"None right now," said Niki.

"Well, as I told you before, we are separating church from outreach. It is all one accounting operation right now, but we will be separating it. Each account has to be separated between church and outreach, the amount determined, then transferred and maintained. You will head up the project of separating the outreach accounts. What I need from you is a monthly report of all outreach and engagement activity. You can be as creative as you would like. This is a copy of the report the way it is prepared now," he said, handing her a file.

Niki skimmed through the report.

"Use it as a guide to create your own report. As you get into the process, you might come up with other ways to present your information," said Vincent. "Overall, you are responsible for the accounting process and financial reporting of outreach activity from beginning to end."

"Who will be working with me?" asked Niki.

"The staff will assist you as you learn the current church processes, but you are it for outreach," said Vincent.

"Where are the controls?" asked Niki.

Vincent, understanding Niki's question from a textbook point of view, asked, "You mean separation of duties type controls?"

"Yes, internal controls, proper accounting procedures," Niki said, trying to understand how this was going to work.

"Using the church as your example, you will establish them on the outreach side. And again, you can be as creative as you want to be. Now, if you don't have any more questions, let's go meet the staff."

They went into the Accounting office. Everyone stopped what they were doing and looked up. Vincent made the introductions.

"This is Sister Nicole Riley, our new outreach accountant. This is Sister Janice Washington, our account analyst, Mary Claiborne, who handles our accounts payable, and Kacy Jenkins, who handles deposits."

Good separation of duties, Niki thought.

They all welcomed her to the department.

"Once you get settled in, I have a special project that I want you involved with. It will get you familiar with the accounts and files. Remember, the goal is for you to head up outreach accounting and finance," Vincent said.

Niki was immediately bombarded with second thoughts about the job. *Me and my big mouth. I better watch what I say because I am getting exactly everything that I said. I don't even like accounting. I just needed to get paid and that is why I even majored in it in the first place. Who goes to college and asks their advisor what do I have to major in to guarantee me a good paying job when I graduate? Somebody who wants to get paid when they graduate, me, that's who. And when the answer was Accounting, I said sign me up so I can get paid. And that ain't even the case here. Oh, well, I'll just look at this as my ministry and they just give me a love offering every week to sow. What degreed, experienced professional accountant doing professional level work makes $25,000? Heck, green, inexperienced, fresh off the stage college graduates with an accounting degree start at $40,000. Somebody must have made a mistake. Show them, Holy Ghost.*

Niki was struggling to overcome the stinging darts of the enemy who wanted her to give up her job before she even started. Realizing that, Niki drew on her faith in God's plan for her life. *I mean, be for real. I just wanted to work for God, serve the people, sweatlessly pay my bills and live a quiet and peaceable life. But I can handle this. It might be fun, especially traveling on engagement. Erica said even before I could object that she would stay with the kids when I have to travel. And between her, Kevin and Randy, I know God hooked this whole thing up.* So Niki resolved to do her absolute very best in setting up the outreach accounting department.

After the completion of the initial project, over the next few weeks Niki was swamped with work. Janice was the first to pass on all outreach accounts to Niki to analyze. Mary was right behind her with all outreach bills to pay. Kacy was more sensitive and held back on giving Niki outreach cash to deposit. The day-to-day operations were getting to Niki. She had not done this detailed level of operations before. She had either audited this type of work or managed the supervisors of the accounting staff who did this type of work. She had been too far removed in her experiences to have dealt with the amount of paper she had to deal with every day. Between the mail, invoices, PO's, checks, deposit slips, reports, and files, it was just too much to keep up with. She had the big picture on her mind all the time and to switch gears to this level of detail took some getting used to. Her experience was more on the management level. Even though she supervised operations in a previous job, she never had to get in there and do the actual work. She had staff to handle that. Here she had to do it all. After it was all said and done, the outreach accounting buck started and stopped with Niki. When the revelation hit her that she was *it*, because she hadn't quite realized the depth before, she knew she had to put the tightest internal controls in place.

While focusing on the checks and balances system of the big picture, sometimes important documents got misplaced or buried in her sea of papers, and she was reprimanded for not being organized.

She thought, *They're just trippin'. Don't they see all this work I got to do?*

She came in at 8:15 one morning and got written up for being consistently late by five to 15 minutes, which she thought was no big deal since she usually stayed an hour to two hours late every day trying to get a handle on that paper.

"What's this?" she asked.

She had never been written up before. Every evaluation she had ever had was always glowing with some type of increase attached to it. Now she was being written up for not punching the clock by 8:00 a.m. Niki had no experience with punching time clocks. She forgot to punch it at all sometimes.

At a staff meeting, Pastor, who was also the CEO of the ministry, addressed the staff. He went over administrative matters and disciplinary issues. He emphasized the importance of being at corporate prayer because it was mandatory that this staff prayed.

"That's what got us here and that is what will take us to where we are going: prayer. You got to pray to work here," Pastor said.

Three write-ups of any kind, including missing corporate prayer outside of the established guidelines, led to suspension. And if you got suspended, you probably wouldn't be back.

Talk about strict. Rules are rules. Niki already had one write-up for being late. She didn't plan on missing any corporate prayers. She'd better walk a tight rope.

Vincent had been pleased with Niki's reports, until one day he asked why a number was so low in one of the outreach accounts. Niki went on to explain that the previous report did not include a certain purchase order that had been overlooked, probably because it had been buried in her mountain of other papers. However, when she found it, she included it in the following report since the purchase order had already been approved. Vincent left, went back to his office, and Niki went back to work. Later, Vincent called Niki into his office and gave her a second write-up which stated that financial decisions were made based on the information she provided and that the information had to be accurate and that there was zero tolerance for error in the accounting department. It went on to say that Niki needed to work on her organization skills to be effective in her position, and that the staff would help her get organized.

Niki thought, *Well, that makes two. One more and I'm outta here. I'll just give Accountants R Us a call when I get home.*

CHAPTER 18

That night, Niki prayed about calling Accountants R Us. She had to do what she had to do for her and her family. She was too realistic to put all her eggs in one basket and what a small basket—$25,000 a year. Surely she was worth double that.

"Lord, you called me here. I know the woman who fed Elijah first didn't run out of food for her and her son, and she was planning to eat what she had and die. Then your prophet came and had the audacity to ask her to feed him. After she told him she didn't have but a little bit, he still asked that she feed him and feed him first. What nerve! Then I realized it must be a test. She passed the test though, and got blessed. And it's because of her example that I know I can live off $25,000, because Pastor is your prophet, ain't no doubt about that. How else does he know to preach all my business?

"But Lord, some of that stuff, the inflexibility, the insensitivity is hard to deal with. I can deal with it better coming from the world because that system is designed to beat you up. And besides, at least the world pays you well and you can go buy yourself something nice to help you forget how bad they treat you. But here at the church, you get written up and then don't have enough money to buy yourself something so you can feel better. Lord, show me what to do so I can feel comfortable and not be paranoid that I'm going to get beat up for every mistake. I don't believe you called me here to feel like this."

There was a knock at the door. It was Kevin.

"You're a sight for sore eyes, a friendly face," she said.

"What's wrong?" asked Kevin.

"I don't know," she said.

"How's work?" he asked.

"I don't know," she answered.

"Oooohh, Lord, come talk to me."

He took her by the hand and led her to the sofa. They sat down on opposite ends of the sofa.

"Now tell me what's going on," he said.

He was the best friend a girl could have. Easy to talk to. Excellent listener. Cool, rational, reasonable, and very mature. Niki told him all about the staff meeting, the write ups and how she thought she might get fired, therefore she had better get her ducks in a row.

"Didn't you sow a $1,000 seed for that job?" he asked.

"Yep," she answered.

Kevin said, "If I pay that much for something, you better bet I ain't giving it up without a fight. And surely nobody is gonna take it from me. Just talk to him, Nik. You're smart, real, open and honest. Let him know exactly how you feel. Then if it doesn't work out, hey, partner, you got the skills to pay the bills," he said.

"I know, but I want to work at the church," she said.

"Then talk to him. Let the Lord lead the conversation. It'll be okay," his encouraging words making her feel 100 percent better.

"You're right. How're you doing?" she turned the conversation onto him.

"My students are a trip. Much going on in the homes that's filtering over into the classroom. But I maintain control regardless. Can't let that slip. I'm getting closer to that contract. Keep praying for me."

"Without ceasing, my brother."

The next day, Niki asked Vincent if she could meet with him.

"Sure," was Vincent's response.

During the meeting Niki shared, "I have prayed and asked God to show me the problem. He didn't. But I just want to talk to you. See, Brother Vincent, I can get a job just about anywhere, but I feel that I am called, anointed, and appointed to be here at this time. I feel comfortable with my position. Of course there is a lot to do, but with all I have to do from beginning to end of the accounting process, surely you don't expect me not to make a mistake. I mean I understand excellence, but you are looking for perfection, and that is just not realistic. People do make mistakes, things get overlooked or misplaced, systems go down, management changes its mind. In the accounting world, timing is everything and we have means, such as adjusted trial balances and notes to the financial statements, to adjust for those types of situations. I believe that if we have the ability to realize our mistakes, analyze and correct them, then that is excellence. For example, I found that purchase order and made correcting adjustments immediately upon recognition of my mistake. I corrected the problem, and due to timing, I included the correction on the following report, and the numbers were accurate. They might not have looked like you wanted them to, but they were accurate. We operate in integrity here. I operated in integrity, and that should be more important than perfection. We all do a lot. Nobody's perfect. I have already resolved to give God my absolute best in this position. Writing me up is not going to make me do a better job because I am already doing my best." She took a deep breath. Then she said, "I just wanted to share that with you. Thank you for the opportunity to get it off my chest."

Vincent took the time to think about what Niki had shared. "Niki, I believe you are called to this position. And I want you here. I think you are doing a good job. I heard every word you said, and I appreciate you talking to me. My door is always open. Let me suggest this. Kacy is very good at organization. Get her to help you get your papers and files organized."

Niki contemplated this.

"I'll do that. Thanks for listening," she said.

On her way back to her desk she thought, *Not one of my co-workers is responsible for the accounting process from beginning to end. The church's duties are properly segregated, and it runs like a fine-tuned clock. Nobody else is building a department, jumping in and out of processes from the detail level to the overall big picture level. They have one job. I have many. And if they are being paid around what I'm being paid, then they are underpaid as well. Lord, I know you are a just God. I just don't get it.*

Kacy helped Niki get her files organized. They went to lunch one day.

"Maybe I'm just not deep enough. I mean, I'm listening to the Morning Show instead of the Word in the mornings, after I pray of course. But I laugh at them fools," said Niki.

"Girl, I listen to them too," confessed Kacy.

"NOOOO, not you," Niki said in shock that Miss Perfect Kacy listened to secular radio.

"They're funny, aren't they? Why can't we?" asked Kacy

"Girl, did you hear The Debate this morning?" asked Niki, feeling closer to Kacy now because of their confessions.

"Yes! I just know people thought I was having a seizure in the car I was laughing so hard," said Kacy.

"Girl, one day they were jamming so hard, then they said 'pull your car over, get out and jam in the street.' I was tempted to do just that. I didn't get out, but I put the car in park at the stoplight and jammed. I was wore out by the time I got to work," said Niki.

"I know what you mean. They are just fun to listen to; I'm sorry if some people can't handle it. They are just funny, okay?" said Kacy.

"Girl, don't let nobody hear you say that too loud, or you'll get written up" said Niki.

"Yeah, right," said Kacy.

They laughed.

Even though Niki did her best, she still made mistakes, but Vincent eased up a lot. She developed an accounting process that had so many checks and balances in it that a fool couldn't mess it up. The Holy Spirit gave it to her in the shower one morning when she was praying for wisdom. When she shared it with Vincent, he was excited because it would give him exactly what Pastor had been asking for. Vincent got the go ahead to hire Niki some help. Things were getting better by the day.

CHAPTER 19

Taj was spending more and more time downstairs. He would go to a football game with the guys on Friday night, and Niki wouldn't see him any more until Sunday. She would call down on Sunday mornings for him to come get ready for church.

"Ma, can I go with Kevin and Randy to 11:00 service? We're still sleepy."

That was fine with Niki. All she required is that he went.

Kevin had joined Way Maker Ministries. Randy liked it a lot but already had a church home and was brought up to believe you never leave your church home. So he just visited Way Maker Ministries often.

She had given them a key to keep down there since the kids were forever losing or leaving theirs. Actually, the guys' apartment had become an extension of her apartment. She could see Taj growing up, and like any mother, she didn't want to let go. He no longer called her "Mommy" or "Mom," but "Ma." Thank God her girls still called her "Mommy." The guys had tactfully let Niki know that boys will be boys and she had to loosen up at some point. *No time soon,* Niki thought. They assured her that she had put the best of everything in her children that they needed in order to live happy, productive lives in Christ. She felt good about her new brothers in Christ and thanked God for them.

She prayed for them always. Especially Kevin, who was working real hard to get his career in education off the ground. Randy's was soaring. He had majored in the right thing. Kevin majored in business and needed a lot more classes to get certified as a teacher. He had joined a fraternity in college and was partying while Randy was studying. Kevin was much more well-rounded though. He was cool, mature, and secure. Randy was a brain, not a nerd though, teaching his students during the day and working on his masters at night. One day Randy showed Niki a letter that one of his students had given him. It read: "I know you are going to think I'm tripping, but I like you for more than a teacher."

"Do you know who wrote it?" asked Niki.

"No, I don't," Randy answered.

"Whatcha gonna do?" she asked.

"Nothing," he said.

"What would you do, Kevin?" she asked.

"Find out who it was and nip it in the bud. I would say, "Look, you are a child, and I am an adult. You are the student, and I am your teacher. You came here to learn and I came here to teach. If you EVER approach me like that again, you will be disciplined. Do you understand?" Kevin said, demonstrating his classroom style.

Kevin's compassion for his students and position commanded respect from his students, peers, and the administration. Niki loved how real he was. She was also very impressed with how he dealt realistically with issues. Randy preferred not to deal with things until he had to.

When Kevin would get his nephew, Rashad, on a weekend, it would be guys weekend. Taj would only come upstairs when he got hungry.

"Mommy, there's no milk," said Maya.

"No way. I just brought some yesterday, and Taj hasn't even been here."

"He took it downstairs," Maya said solving the mystery of the disappearing milk.

"What?"

"He took the cereal, too," she snitched.

"Those guys," said Niki, shaking her head. "Oh, well. I'll pick some up later."

There was a knock on the door. It was Randy holding a grocery bag with something in it with both hands.

"Hi, Niki."

"Hey, Randy."

"Will you please cook this for us?"

Niki peeked in the bag. It was a huge pot roast.

"Put it in the sink," she said stepping back to let him pass, pointing towards the kitchen.

"How long will it take?" he asked.

"A while."

"We have a flag football game at three o'clock. We should be back by about five or six. You think it'll be ready by then?"

"Oh, yeah," she said.

"Okay, then. We have Taj and Rashad with us. Thanks, Niki. Catch you later."

"You got it, man."

And that's how it was. One big happy family.

The kids went to Virginia to spend the holidays with Sam. It was the first Christmas ever that Niki did not spend with her family. As a matter of fact, she spent it with Jesus chilling in front of a roaring fire, blankets all over the floor, video tapes in front of the large screen TV. She was in heaven and couldn't remember ever feeling this good, safe, secure, and at total peace. Jesus was in this place and she just basked in His glory, thanking Him for all that was happening in her life, her job, and the wonderful people He had surrounded her with.

She hung out at the throne of God for Christmas. There was a knock at the door. *Dag.* She got up, and it was Kevin. Hair sticking up all over her head, flannel pajamas, she opened the door part way and didn't say anything.

"How're you doing up here all by yourself?"

"Just fine, and I am never alone. Jesus is all up in here with me," she said.

"Good, just checking on you. Here's a card we got for you," he said handing it to her through the partially opened door.

"Oh, that's so sweet. I got y'all something too," she said taking the card and opening the door all the way so he could come in.

She went to her bedroom to get it, and he came into the apartment. He stopped suddenly in his tracks. He looked around and saw books, pillows, blankets, tapes all over the floor and the blazing fire. He thought it was the most romantic sight he had ever seen, like a scene out of a movie. It was warm and cozy and he got a funny feeling in the pit of his stomach.

Niki came back and handed him the small gift.

"Nothing much, just a little some'n, some'n to let you know I really appreciate you guys."

Kevin took it and looked at Niki. At that precise moment, she was the most beautiful woman he had ever seen, nappy head, flannel pajamas and all.

Niki said, "Well, I got to get back to Jesus."

"Oh, okay. Glad you're doing alright without the kids. Call us if you need anything."

He walked slowly down the stairs trying to figure out what just happened.

The break was good for Niki. She and Erica hung out all over Zion. She hung out with Tina, too. But mostly she hung out at the throne. The guys checked on her every day. They brought her dinner and just took real good care of her. She did miss her kids though.

When they got back home, they needed a truck to get everything in that they had gotten for Christmas. She had a lot of gifts to open herself that loved ones had sent from home.

Work was good. She hadn't been late at all while the kids were gone. She concluded that it was taking them to the bus stop and waiting with them until the bus came that was the problem. No way was she leaving her children at the bus stop, especially since it was still dark. She explained the situation to Vincent and asked that her hours be changed so that she could come in 15 minutes later and leave 15 minutes later. Vincent agreed. That 15 minutes made a big difference. It was a stroke of genius since Niki was never late again, although she had one close call. It was one morning when everything was going like usual. But that day, when she dropped the kids off on the narrow street where the bus stopped, she did something really stupid. Impatiently, she backed up to make a U-turn in the street so that she didn't have to wait for the bus to move but could go on to work in the opposite direction. When she backed up, she slipped into a ditch. Now she was stuck in the ditch on a side road, and the bus was taking off. She didn't know what to do. She sure couldn't lift a car out of a ditch. So she sat there, closed her eyes and prayed.

"Father, look what I have done. I'm so impatient. I need your help, Father. Please get me out of this ditch, in Jesus' name, Amen."

The prayer took all of three seconds. When Niki opened her eyes, she saw two black men in white uniforms and caps walking towards her car from a white truck that was parked across the street. They walked to the back of Niki's car, lifted it out of the ditch, waved to her and went back and got in the truck and pulled off. She waved and yelled "Thank you" out the window. That took all of 30 seconds. In less than a minute, God had answered Niki's prayer.

As she praised the Lord on her way to work she tried to remember what company the guys worked for. She couldn't, for the life of her, picture the logo on the uniform. So she tried to remember the sign on the truck and couldn't. All she remembered seeing was white. She tried and tried and tried. Nothing on their caps. Just white. Then it hit her. Those weren't men—those were her angels! Manifested in the flesh to help and protect her. She had seen her angels. She was overwhelmed. She cried and praised God all the way to work.

When she got to work she told everybody she saw. "I saw my angels. They manifested to help me this morning." The people she told were fascinated because they, too, believed in angels. She couldn't wait until the kids got home to tell them, and of course she had to tell the guys.

When she was telling Kevin, he was looking at her funny.

"What's wrong? You don't believe me?" she asked him.

Of course, I believe you, Niki, he thought. *I believe you, I believe in you, I think you are wonderful, I think you're beautiful, I think you're exciting, I think I love you. Oh, God, what a predicament.*

CHAPTER 20

Kevin had been looking strange lately. Niki recognized the look, but didn't want to admit it. That would just mess everything up. *Besides he's too young.* Maybe she should get that new book that's out which is supposed to deal with this sort of thing. Kevin never said anything to her, but she knew because a woman knows when a man feels like that. Must be some kind of vibe or something. It was driving her crazy. She needed to talk to Erica.

"Let's do lunch. I have to talk to you about something," Niki said when she called Erica upon arriving to work.

"Okay," Erica agreed.

At noon, as they walked to the lobby, a woman stood up and greeted Erica. Erica introduced her to Niki as Sister Jada, a volunteer.

"Sister Jada will be joining us for lunch," said Erica.

Niki was furious. She wanted to discuss Kevin with Erica. Not with Erica *and* Jada. Who is Sister Jada anyway?

Niki didn't say two words through lunch. She let them talk. She hoped she wasn't pouting; but if she was, she didn't care. She needed to talk about Kevin. They talked about where Jada would be volunteering in the ministry.

Send her to distribution so I can sic my boys on her. Make 'em pledge her interrupting-my-lunch, who-she-think-she-is butt. I guess she's all right. I just need to talk about Kevin, Niki thought.

Thursday was Chinese buffet day for Niki and Chris. This week it was Niki's turn to drive. Chris knew to be ready at twelve noon. Niki was running late from a meeting that ran overtime. At 12:10 she called Chris.

"I'm on my way," she said and hung the phone up before he could get a word in edgewise.

When she pulled up in front of the promotions department, Niki was shocked.

Oh no, not her again, she thought.

Not only did Chris get in Niki's car, but so did Sister Jada.

What the heck is her problem? Niki thought.

"I told Sister Jada we were having Chinese, and she wanted to come. She said she knew you. I didn't think you would mind," said Chris.

She must not know me if she's jumping in my car like she's crazy, Niki thought having flashbacks of the hood she grew up in. "No, that's fine," Niki lied. *Forgive me, Father.*

As they ate, Niki decided to make the best of the situation.

"So where are you from, Sister Jada?"

"Boston. And you?"

"Fulton, Virginia."

"I lived in Fulton for five years."

"Really? What church did you go to?" asked Niki.

"The Assemblies of God," said Jada.

"I went to the Fulton Christian Center. I've been to plays at the Assemblies though."

"I was in the Christmas and Easter productions."

"They were wonderful. The kids and I thoroughly enjoyed them."

"How many children do you have?" Jada asked.

"Three. Two girls and a boy. Do you have any?"

"I have twin boys. Eric and Elijah," said Jada.

"Wow. Did you and your husband trip?"

"I'm divorced. And the boys are the best things that ever happened to me."

"I feel the same way about my children. I don't know what I would do without them sometimes. How old are they?"

"They are 16 and I am so proud of them. They are straight "A" students and they both want to be lawyers like their mother."

"You're a lawyer?" Niki asked, shocked and impressed.

"Attorney Ross at your service. I have to take the Georgia bar in a couple of months to practice here. I'm studying now, and I'm volunteering at the church to get away from the books, to do something different and positive for the Lord before I go stir crazy," said Jada.

"I know what you mean, girl."

Niki was beginning to like Jada more and more. Jada was cool people, a little bourgie maybe, but Niki liked the way she talked and carried herself. She was okay. Niki forgave her for interrupting her lunch...twice.

Chris was enjoying his meal. He let them talk and thanked God that Niki seemed not to be upset with him anymore.

Work was going really well. Niki had more and more freedom, and her ideas were accepted and implemented. Engagement season was about to begin; therefore, she began to travel with the team. When they got to the cities, Niki was fascinated watching the people. They really showed their love of God and for the ministry through their giving. Niki had her work cut out for her on the road. But she had a wonderful, experienced team who made her life easy. The entire team was great and flowed together as one, and the people got blessed city after city after city. She always brought T-shirts back. The kids had shirts from most of the major cities.

Back home, between Erica and Kevin, the kids had a blast. They didn't even miss Niki that much because at least Erica entertained them. She took them out to do fun stuff. The big kids loved bowling and skating. She let Mia get all made up and put on lots and lots of lipstick. Mia loved lipstick and now, thanks to Erica's teaching, she could put it on perfectly. Then after she was all glamorous, Erica would introduce her as Little Miss Mia Hollywood. She'd make a grand entrance, almost trip and fall in Erica's high heels and take a bow while they all applauded and laughed at her dramatics.

Kevin took them to the movies. He liked the kind of movies they liked. They much preferred going with him than with their mother.

Niki was having just as much fun out on the road. They ate at nice restaurants, stayed in nice plush hotels, but the biggest thrill of all was watching the people respond to Pastor. They literally pulled the Word out of him.

One service, Pastor, being his old funny self, was making the point of how important it is to be at a church that is feeding you the Word and not just a lot of emotionalism.

"You shout, cry, dance 'til you sweat, then the preacher gets up there and preaches ET Phone Home," he said.

The congregation roared. Then he preached it.

"When was the last time you PHONED HOME?"

They fell back in their chairs in laughter.

"You know, every now and then you need to…PHONE HOME," Pastor preached in his heaviest, deepest, countriest, black southern baptist voice.

The congregation, now hysterical, was slapping the backs of the chairs.

"When your baby needs a new pair of shoes, why don'tcha…PHONE HOME. When your phone is disconnected, you need to…PHONE HOME."

Some were on the floor now. Niki thought, *That doesn't even make sense. How you gonna phone home when your phone is disconnected? But look at these people. They love him.* He was funny though.

"And you waiting on your next paycheck…PHONE HOME"

Niki saw one woman slide all the way down in her seat in a fit of laughter, and the woman beside her had her head laid on her chest laughing uncontrollably.

"AAAHHHHHHHHH LOOK! You got a light bill due…PHONE HOME."

The place went wild. Then in the midst of it all, Pastor brought it home. "And those same people leave church, still in debt, still in bondage, still defeated because nobody was teaching them THE WORD OF THE LIVING GOD!" And the place went quiet. He had them. In the palm of his hand. All they wanted right here, right now was the Word of the living God. And he poured it in them. Niki watched it time and time again. The people were being set free across the country, and she was a part of this mighty move of God. She was humbled to be chosen. She had learned that many are called but few were chosen. It was those that showed up that were chosen. She had shown up in Zion, now look. *God is an awesome God.*

When she got back, she talked with Erica. Now would be a good time to tell her about Kevin.

"You know, you're our guardian angel. I don't know what I would do without you, girl. Thanks for staying with the kids," said Niki.

"The kids are great, Niki. We have a ball. It is a pleasure to stay with them," Erica said.

"Girl, I have been trying to tell you something forever. But we've been so busy and I had to travel. It's about Kevin." Erica looked at Niki.

"Girl, he's changing. He's looking all funny," said Niki.

"What do you expect as nice as you've been to that boy?" asked Erica.

"That boy has been nice to me. We are like family."

"What did he say?" asked Erica.

"He hasn't said anything to me. So maybe I'm just imagining things, right?" asked Niki hopefully, her life being almost perfect right now.

"Wrong. They don't have to say anything to us women. We just know. If you think he has developed a crush on you, then he probably has. But you're okay because you're still married," said Erica.

"Yeah, I am. And that's another story. I need to know what to do with that. I got to pray," said Niki.

"Then go talk to Minister Thornhill. He's anointed in that area. I've gotta go. I'll see you tomorrow," said Erica.

"Bye and thanks again for everything."

Niki prayed that night, "Lord tell me what You want me to do about this marriage to Sam. Clearly I have gone on with my life and am so happy and at peace. I don't want to go back, and he said he is never coming here. Give me wisdom and direction, Lord, in Jesus' name. Amen."

The next day Niki went in to talk to Minister Thornhill.

"Minister Thornhill, my marriage is in limbo. That's not a good state to be in. It's a constant state of not knowing. I want to know what God is going to do about my marriage," said Niki.

"What do you want?" asked Minister Thornhill.

"God's best," she said, trying to sound deep.

"And what is that?"

"I don't know. I know He hates divorce."

"So what do you want?"

"All I want is for God's will to be done in my life."

"What do you think that is?"

"I don't know. But He hates divorce," she said, feeling like she was getting nowhere.

Sensing her frustration, Minister Thornhill asked, "Do you want your marriage?"

"To be totally honest with you, Minister Thornhill, I would have to say not anymore."

"And you said you wanted God's best for your life, correct?"

"Yes, sir."

"Do you believe God's best for you is your marriage?"

Good question, she thought. *I have put God in a box. God's best is what's best for me, and clearly this marriage to this man is not God's best for me.*

"Praise God. I see it now, Minister Thornhill. Thank you."

"Praise the Lord, Sister."

She left his office feeling 100 pounds lighter now with the realization that she was not bound to her marriage to Sam. It was like a burden was removed from off her shoulder, and the yoke of bondage was removed from her neck. Minister Thornhill is definitely anointed, just like Isaiah said.

She called Sam, who was still pouting after all this time because she had physically left him, although he had mentally left her long before.

"What do you want to do?" she asked him.

She was shocked to hear him say, "Divorce me." He felt she had abandoned him when he was down. The marriage was over for him at that point. *Isn't that just like a drug addict? Always the victim.*

She filed for a quick divorce since it was uncontested. Now all she had to do was wait for the final decree, and she would be free. That thought excited her for some reason.

Jada called her to go to lunch. Niki shared about her pending divorce, and Jada could relate to it. They had become real close. They talked about getting the children together.

Jada stopped by with the boys to meet Niki and the kids. Introductions were made all around.

"Want to play some basketball?" Taj asked the twins.

They both looked at their mother, who looked at Niki.

"That's fine. Stop downstairs and see if Kevin will go with you," said Niki.

While the girls played in their room, Jada and Niki sat and talked while the guys walked to the basketball court.

Taj and Eric teamed up against Kevin and Elijah. The twins were more academically than athletically inclined. Kevin and Elijah won, but not without an apparent struggle. Kevin was a good motivational coach. They had a great time.

When they went back to the apartment, Kevin looked at Niki and his heart did a summersault. "I'm going to go downstairs and get cleaned up. Good game, guys. We'll give you a chance to redeem yourselves one day soon," Kevin teased looking at Eric, then at Taj, while giving Elijah five. "This old man still got enough in him to do more than just coach."

Kevin recognized the twins for the strong intellectuals and weak athletes they were. Next time he would team up with Eric so that Eric could have a chance to win. Never would he team up with Taj against the twins. That would just be too unfair, too unbalanced, in spite of the age difference. Without grace, mercy, or a miracle, the twins would surely get skunked.

"Cool," said Eric.

Elijah was just grinning, feeling extremely proud.

"Nice meeting you, Jada. Niki, call me later when your company leaves, no matter how late." He had to tell her tonight how he felt. He couldn't hold it back, not one more day.

After Jada and the twins had left and the kids were all tucked in, Niki called downstairs.

"Hello," said Kevin.

"What's up?" she said.

Recognizing her voice, he asked, "Can I come up just for a minute?" He had to face this music.

"Okay."

Five seconds later, he was in the apartment facing Niki. He scanned the apartment for the kids and concluded that they were down for the night, so this was the best time to do this.

After they settled down on the couch, he began, "I don't know when it happened, but I am in love with you. I'm sorry. I didn't mean for it to happen, but it did and I can't keep it to myself any longer," Kevin said with a slightly desperate tone, yet his cool still reigning.

Niki was in shock. She knew it, but to hear it was different. "I'm married," she said, not having shared with him about her pending divorce to Sam.

"I understand. I'm gonna go. I just had to tell you. I'm sorry."

He left. Niki shut the door and ran in her room and prayed. "Lord, what in the world is going on? Are you setting me up? I'm just gonna sit tight."

Niki, Erica and Jada went out for dessert and coffee after service. Niki told them that Kevin had told her he was in love with her.

97

"What's he gonna do?" asked Erica.

"What does he have to offer?" asked Jada.

She was really getting upset with these materialistic sisters of hers.

"Where does he work?" asked Erica.

"How old is he?" Jada said on her turn.

"He better go get somebody he can handle," said Erica.

"He has been handling me. He's got goals, dreams, vision," replied Niki.

"Does he have any money, houses, cars?" asked Jada.

"Chile, please. You will hurt that boy," said Erica.

"I don't know. He looks capable to me," defended Niki.

"You just spent too much time together," said Jada.

"Never alone, though," said Niki.

"Girl, forget that. You need a *man* to help you with those kids. He's a good friend and all, but your rich prince might be right around the corner," said Erica.

"That's you, Cinderella. I can take care of me and my babies and don't need no man for that."

"She's got a point, Erica. I lived in a mansion, and we slept in separate bedrooms, so I hear ya, Nik. I feel the same way. But still, he's got to come bearing gifts. I mean nice ones," said Jada.

"You both are going to be waiting on your knights or princes or Peter Pan, for all I care, for a long time. This brother has established something deeper than all that with me and my family. I'm going to see what he's talking about," said Niki, frustrated.

"You do that and let us know what he's bringing to the table. And if you think about it, you can figure out yourself that it's probably not much, and Niki you deserve so much more. We are virtuous women, and our price is far above rubies. Read Proverbs, girl," said Erica.

"You might be right. But that's not what's important to me. You got all types of women. Some say, 'You take care of me, baby, pay all the bills, handle everything, and all I'll do is serve you.' No offense, Erica, but I want to throw up on that type of woman," said Niki.

"It would work for me," said Erica.

Niki continued, "Then there are the rich ones who don't need a man's money, just his presence. Kinda like the flip side of the first one. Don't know what I'd do if I had that kind of money." Niki thought about it for a split second, "Naww, I ain't never taking care of no man. Then there's the type that does everything with her man. Work with him, sleep with him, play with him. I would get really sick of him, okay? Then there's the Equal Partner type. You take care of your business, and let me take care of mine. Split everything down the middle. Guess that's what you call a balanced relationship."

"Door number one, baby. Take care of me," said Erica.

"See, now that's why you had to go to the hospital diving for that bouquet at Diane's wedding, like it was going to sho' nuff get you a husband," said Niki.

"Don't go there," said Erica, "my side still hurts."

"The way that girl tackled you for that bouquet, you need to let me send that tape to Funny Home Movies. Then you'll have enough money so you can stop tripping and get a real man and not waste your time waiting for a fairy tale prince," Niki unleashed.

"See, she went there, Jada," said Erica.

"Yes, you did, Niki, now apologize," said Jada.

"I apologize to the wide receiver. But you went for that pass and she tackled your…"

"NIKI!" they yelled.

CHAPTER 21

Jada was in the library studying for the bar. She was frustrated because a particular reference book she needed was already being used. As she sat and scanned the crowded library, deep in thought about opening her own firm, a brother sat down at the table with her. This further annoyed her until she spotted the book she was looking for among his things.

"May I see that book, please?" she asked.

"Sorry, sister, I'm about to use it. I had to give up my driver's license to get it from the librarian, and you think I am just going to hand it over to you? I don't even know you," he said, teasing.

She laughed at his humor. She clearly wasn't thinking.

"I understand, brother. But when you finish with it, I'm next, okay?"

"You need to ask the librarian about that because I'm putting it back where I got it from so I can drive myself home," he said.

"Touché again."

She must be tired because that was the second dumb thing she had said to this fine brother. He must think she's an idiot. She should just keep her mouth shut for the rest of the day. She just sat there quietly contemplating what to do while she waited for the book.

"My name is Mark Alexander."

"Jada Ross," she said, keeping it short before she said something else crazy.

"Are you an attorney, Jada?" asked Mark knowing that only lawyers or law students would even know this book existed. Jada appeared to be too sophisticated to be a student in spite of the way she tried to get his book.

"Yes, I am, Mark. What about you?"

"Yes, licensed in Maryland, however. I am studying for the Georgia bar."

"Massachusetts here. And I'm doing the same thing," said Jada.

"Well, much success to you," Mark said, not believing in luck.

Mark was a firm believer in "You reap what you sow." If one worked hard and honest, applying faith pressure no matter what happened and didn't let up, that is what caused the desired results to manifest. Oh, he believed in the mercy and grace of God that saved people from what they did deserve and gave them what they didn't deserve. He even believed in the favor of God, but people had

100

responsibility for their own fate, and he left nothing to chance. He worked hard for what he wanted, and right now he wanted to go into private practice.

"I receive it in the name of Jesus," said Jada.

Wait a minute. That wasn't lawyer talk. That was faith talk. Mark looked at Jada. He saw it. There's just something about people who have the Holy Spirit living on the inside of them.

"Praise the Lord, Sister," he said.

"Praise Him," she answered.

"You're saved, aren't you?" he asked.

"Saved, sanctified, and filled with the Holy Ghost," she said.

"What about tongue talking, Bible believing?" he asked.

"All that. What about you?" asked Jada.

"Absolutely. Completely sold out for Jesus," said Mark.

"Well, all right," said Jada. "We have something in common. What church do you attend?" she asked.

"Way Maker Ministries. What about you?" he asked.

"No place else to be for me. The Word is so tight. No way around it. Just do it and get results. And that's what I'm after, results in Jesus," she said.

"My sentiments exactly," he said. "I'll include you in my prayers for sweatless victory over the bar, and you do the same for me, okay?"

"You got it, Brother. Nice meeting you," she said.

"Same here," he said. Not seeing a wedding band, he felt an urging to know more about her. "What service do you go to, Jada?"

"Usually 7:00 and, of course, weekly Bible study," she answered.

"Me, too," he said.

Boldly and confidently, he continued, "Would you like to go to breakfast after service tomorrow?" he asked.

Jada liked his directness. A man who didn't beat around the bush. She was interested. A brother in Christ with whom she had something in common. This should prove to be very interesting. He might even have some ideas and insights on how she should start her own firm God's way.

"Sure, Mark. That would be nice."

"Great. Meet me in the lobby after service?"

"I'll be looking for you," she said.

They had a wonderful time at breakfast. They discussed the legal system and their professional experiences. The conversation was refreshing, easy but deep. They wanted to continue, but Jada needed to get home to the boys. They made plans to continue the conversation later on in the week.

After Bible study that Wednesday, they went to a restaurant for fellowship and to pick up where they had left off Sunday. They both were interested in the other's ideas on starting a godly legal practice. They had felt a connection from the very first time they met. Now the conversation turned personal. Jada inspired him to open up. Mark told her all about his ex, daughter, parents, siblings, growing up in Maryland, college and how he came to Way Makers Ministries. Jada told him all about her ex, twins, family in Boston, and how when she was in Zion on business an associate suggested that she visit Way Makers Ministries. Time flew. They made plans for Mark to come by Jada's to check out her law library and meet the boys.

"I'll come by after the celebration, since we'll be at church all next week," he said.

"Sure, that will work out perfectly," she said, since her and her sisters had the whole celebration week planned.

It was time to celebrate the completion of the new facility. People came from all over to join in the festivities. Top named ministers from around the world came to minister the Word of God along with Grammy award winning music ministry gifts. It was a power-packed, anointed extravaganza.

"I don't know how much more excitement I can stand," Niki told her sisters over dessert and coffee after one of the celebration services.

"Just getting you ready for Jesus, Nik. Getting us ready to be caught up in the air," said Erica.

"This is nothing compared to the glorious time *that* will be," said Jada.

"Oh, yes, amen," said Niki on a serious high from all the excitement. She was having an absolute ball in her new land.

Erica received several invitations from suitors interested in her. Some just wanted to spend time with her. Some wanted to get to know her. Some seriously wanted to take a shot at making her their mate. She accepted a few invitations to go out.

"Any prospects, Erica?" asked Niki.

"Why the ones with the money got to be eyeballing me? I ain't but five foot two, so what does that make them if they are short enough to look me in the eye without stooping, leaning, or bending?"

Niki and Jada were cracking up.

"I refuse to answer that," said Niki.

"Don't look at me," said Jada.

"Then why the sho' nuff fine ones, slick as Crisco, trying to act saved or broke?" asked Erica.

"I don't know," said Niki, about to burst.

"Me neither," said Jada, trying seriously to suppress a laugh.

"Not one real prospect in the bunch. Lord, where is my man?" cried Erica.

"Careful, girl, you sound desperate. Did Jada tell you about Brother Mark?"

"Brother who?" asked Erica.

"He's got it going on, girl. A lawyer with goals of going into private practice and building a successful, not to mention lucrative, law practice. Now who that sound like?" asked Jada.

"That would be you, girl. Now you got a man. Niki got a man. Where's my man?" cried Erica.

"Wait a minute. Wait one darn minute. I do not, and I repeat, I *do not have* a man, *nor do I want* a man. I am currently waiting to be divorced from a man, and that is the story with me and a man," said Niki.

"And I just met a man. I'm talking to the man. However, I don't have a man yet either. So you are not the only one manless," said Jada.

"But she's the only one who has a problem with it. They could all disappear as far as I'm concerned, and I wouldn't even go look for them," Niki said.

"I wouldn't even ask, 'Where they at?'" Jada said and gave Niki high five.

Ignoring her sisters' nonchalant comments, Erica said, "Well, at least y'all got prospects to talk about."

"Since when do you care about talk as cheap as it is, Sister Expensive? Remember you're holding out for your rich knight in shining armor, so you got to sacrifice the talk. You can't have it all. So, Jada, my man's at home with the kids, where's your man tonight?" Niki said, teasing.

"Leave me alone, girl," Erica said laughing.

Mark and Jada were spending a lot of time together, studying and talking about private law practice. The conversation had turned to them being partners. Jada, being the organized visionary, wrote it all down. It looked great on paper. They couldn't deny the potential, especially with their faith and talent in the mix. They decided that they had what it took to pull it off. They agreed to do it.

Mark and Jada had done a great job of avoiding the obvious physical attraction between them because of their being focused on the bar, the practice, and the Word of God. However, now that they both were licensed in Georgia and that burden had been removed, Jada could feel herself falling for him. The attraction got the best of them, and they found themselves in an awkward position. Jada couldn't risk anything happening between them so she began to push him away. Being the conservative, uncompromising, strong, in-control woman that she was, she started thinking that things were moving just a little bit too fast. Therefore, she suggested that they chill for a while so that she could clear her thinking. Mark, being as fine, intelligent and sought after as he was, couldn't deal with rejection and thought, *Well, fine then.* So he stopped calling.

After one service Jada ran into an old beau in the lobby. "Lamar Price. What are you doing here?"

"Jada Ross. Will wonders never cease!"

They hooked up, and he treated her like the lady she was. He knew her, her taste, her style. He wined and dined her, buying her gifts. She enjoyed the treatment. However, she was now subconsciously using him to get her mind off of Mark. She had fallen in love with him and realized it too late. Lamar was doing a good job of distracting her, but not completely. Mark had made a strong impression.

When she and Lamar walked into church together one Sunday, they ran into Mark. Jada introduced them.

"Brother Lamar, this is Brother Mark."

The men spoke and shook hands. Then Jada and Lamar turned and walked into the sanctuary, leaving Mark standing back in a daze. It did not go unnoticed by Lamar that they had feelings for each other. The tension was thick enough to cut.

Mark was furious, so he decided to date a couple of the ladies from the church. That plan backfired because they just made him miss Jada more since nobody could measure up.

He prayed for humility, bit the bullet, and called Jada.

"I need to talk to you. Can I please come over?"

"Sure," Jada said coolly.

When he got there, she was watching TV. The boys were up in their room.

"I want to apologize for being a jerk," he said.

"Whatever do you mean?" asked Jada.

"You did the right thing by backing up when you felt we were moving too fast," he said.

"When did you get that revelation?" she asked, knowing good and well Lamar helped him get it.

"Doesn't matter. The point is, I got it," he said.

"Fine."

He paused, trying to come up with the best way to say what he wanted to say. He decided to just say it. Smart as she was, she probably already knew what he wanted to say.

"I believe we are good together, Jada," he said.

She wasn't going to make it easy.

"Maybe we could have been, but I'm seeing Lamar now."

Mark had to find some extra strength to push all his pride aside. He couldn't remember being in this type of position before.

"But what about the practice?"

"Honey, I am doing what I was doing before I met you. Surely you didn't think I was sitting around waiting on you, do you?" she asked.

"But I know we can build an awesome practice together," he said, no longer convinced that he could do it without her.

"And your point is?" asked Jada.

Completely ignoring her comment about Lamar, he confessed, "I have been miserable without you. I want us to build a practice and a life together," he said.

Thank you, Father, she prayed silently, rejoicing on the inside, cooler than a cucumber on the outside. She decided to let him sweat for a night or two before she told him how much she loved and missed him so he would think twice before trying that foolishness again.

"Mark, I have to pray about what you have shared with me tonight. I'll give you a call in a couple of days. Thank you for stopping by. Have a good evening," she said, getting up and walking towards the door.

He left shaken, not knowing if he had blown it with her or not. He had to go home and pray like he had never prayed before.

When Lamar had asked her about Mark, she was honest with him about her feelings. Even though he still loved her, a real man knows when to back away. They agreed to be friends and wished each other the best.

Jada went to the throne of God and got a plan for how this would work with Mark. They had children, ex's and in-laws to consider. She wrote down her plan to make it plain so they could run with it. Mark hadn't heard anything from Jada in two days. On the third day she called and asked him to come over. She gave Mark her plan. He read it and looked at her.

"I can live with this," he said.

CHAPTER 22

Kevin was pacing the floor of his apartment after he had returned from sharing his true feelings with Niki. *Did he really tell her he loved her to her face? Whew! It was a relief to get it off his chest. But now what?* He had to talk to Randy.

"Randy, man, I'm in love with Niki."

"Duh. So what else is new?"

"What do you mean?" asked Kevin.

"Man you got to be deaf, dumb, and blind not to have seen that coming. You just about live up there. The kids live down here. You dropped Traci like a hot potato right after Niki moved here, and you started going up there."

"That wasn't working with Traci and was just about over anyway."

"Yeah, okay. But Miss Niki helped it to be over quicker. So what are you gonna do?"

"I already did."

"What? What did you do?"

"I told her."

"You told her what?"

"That I was in love with her."

"You did what?! You done lost your mind! I can't believe you told that woman with all those kids that. Why didn't you just ride it out? It would have passed. Now you done opened your big mouth. Dag, man, you dumb. You done messed up. She's probably up there laughing at your young stupid butt right now. What did she say?" lectured Randy.

"Nothing. Guess she had to think about it," Kevin said sadly.

Randy shook his head, "Dumb, man, just dumb."

Kevin looked confused, hurt, stupid. Overlooking the insults from his insensitive roommate—that was just Randy's way—he was deep in thought. He didn't know what was going on. *Clearly this was not in my plan. I have a lot to do. Falling in love, especially with this woman, was not in the plan.* He tried in vain to deny his feelings. He had carried the burden around for months trying to put his feelings in check. Every time he saw her, a love that he had never experienced before bubbled up from way down deep. He was helpless. It wouldn't go away. Obviously Randy had never experienced this type of love before, or he would not be saying those things. He was not a good person to talk to about this because he didn't understand.

Reading Kevin's thoughts, Randy said, "Look, man. You my boy. Whatever you want to do, you know I'm with you. I just want you happy. If that's what you want, go for it. I'm there for you. Whatever, man. Do what you got to do."

"I appreciate that, man. You will always be my boy. Maybe I should just ride it out and see what happens. Only thing with that is I've been riding it out for months. I figured out when it hit me, too. When I went up there to check on her at Christmas, she had it so romantic up in there, fire, warm and cozy atmosphere. What got me is that she was perfectly content all by herself. I wanted to jump down on that floor and snuggle up with her so bad right then and there. Don't get me wrong. I would never disrespect that woman. She is too special for me to even think about approaching her like that. But everything else we had—the loyalty, the trust, the communication—we were handling that on the friendship level. But that night took me to a level that a mere friendship couldn't deal with. It was really intimate in there, and I wanted to know her on that level. I still do."

"Isn't she still married?" asked Randy.

"And that, too. She has said that she doesn't know what's going to happen to her marriage, although left up to her and as far as she is concerned, it's over. She wants to move on with her life. God is going to have to work that out or take these feelings away from me."

"How does she feel about you?" asked Randy.

"You know, she is a lady first and foremost. She carries herself that way and treats me with nothing less than the utmost respect, as I do her. She doesn't look or say anything to me out of the way, to lead me on or let me know she's interested in me that way, intentionally. But sometimes, and I'm sure it is subconscious, but I catch her looking at me like more than a brother. She's a Christian without a doubt. But she's also a red-blooded, warm-bodied woman. Through no fault of her own, I have seen a sensuous woman through her Christianity, and it is extremely attractive. To be honest, the combination is irresistible," explained Kevin.

"Well, whatcha gonna do, man?" asked Randy.

"I've done all I can do. I've told her how I feel. The ball is now in her court. And, knowing Niki, she can handle a ball."

Since all she had to do was wait for her final decree to be completely divorced from Sam, Niki felt a little free to entertain some thoughts about Kevin. Not Kevin her brother in Christ; Kevin her man. *No, no, no. I don't need a man hanging around stopping other men from blessing me.* She had a blast with brothers from the church, going to lunch, dinner, movies, or just hanging. They also treated her like a damsel in distress, those who knew she was a single mother. One of the security guys asked her, "When's the last time you checked the oil in your car?" She just looked up in the air. "Give me your keys," he said. He came back later, handed her the keys and said "I put two quarts in. That will hold you for a while." "How much do I owe you?" she asked. "Nada. Just remember to have it checked from time to time."

Pastor really trained the men well. She felt well taken care of, and a boyfriend would definitely mess that up if he wasn't willing to do all of that. She wasn't sure. Kevin hadn't asked about her oil. She's sure if she asked him to check it for her he would, but she wasn't comfortable doing that. If he offered, she would certainly accept though. But he's not her boyfriend either. Her man would have to take responsibility for that without her asking if she was going to cut off her fellowship with other men. And what would be the point anyway? What would she be able to do with Kevin as her boyfriend that she couldn't do with him as her friend? Like Pastor asked the teens: "What do you mean 'you go together'? What is the difference between 'being friends' and 'going together' to a Christian?" That is what Niki wanted to know as well. To the world, going together meant 'sleeping with.' That could only happen in marriage if you are seriously striving to walk upright before the Lord. She had all the other benefits under the umbrella of friendship. Everything was cool.

Then she did something she dared not do. Something she was avoiding, running from. *Only for a moment won't hurt,* she thought. She decided to entertain the thought of being married to Kevin, then quickly changed her mind. *If I go there, I might not come back.* But she couldn't be afraid to deal with her true feelings. *What if he wanted to marry me? Naw, no, heck no. Don't even think about it. NO! Don't entertain the thought. Cast down that evil imagination in the name of Jesus. He is too, too, too young. You have none, zilch, not even a little bit of patience to deal with a baby Christian. You will be unequally yoked. You understand the things of God because you have been taught well, and contrary to popular belief unequally yoked doesn't just mean saved vs. unsaved, but it could also mean baby vs. mature Christian. Won't work girl. It just will not work. Forget about it.*

Well, let's see. He has grown tremendously in the things of God since we first met. We know each other, we have loyalty, trust, friendship, communication, and I must admit I love his fine butt now that the darn cat is out of the bag. He's got dreams, goals, vision and is not just sitting around talking about them, but is working on them. If he was my age, he would be there, and I do have a ten year jump on the brother to consider. He's no nonsense, and the icing on the cake is he can sing. Sweetest voice I've ever heard. I like that. Is that You, God? Little extra special touches that you know I like to let me know that's You? Well, if it is, I would need my space. I got my own dreams and goals. I want to write. I don't see where our individual dreams and goals will interfere with the other's. So that could work. Money is nice, but trust is a lot nicer and I trust him. Well, let's just say I trust him more than I have ever trusted any other man. As long as he can take care of himself.

The scariest thought in the world to Niki was to be totally dependent on a man to meet her material needs. She knew men who controlled their women with that, and the women were powerless to do anything or go anywhere when the men started acting up. The women would have to stay there and take the abuse. She would never ever be in that kind of a situation. Jean taught her that. She believed with all her heart that her mother had more money than her dad stashed away somewhere that they will never know about. Niki called it being smart. That was one area she had to constantly pray about. Even if she doesn't have the money, a woman should at least have the courage, strength, and faith in God to know that she will make it if she has to quickly exit a bad situation. Having her own money makes it easier. She shouldn't let it get to the point where she feels trapped to stay because her self esteem and self worth have been nullified by a controlling man. *I have never met a man, heard of a man, read about a man in a book, or seen a man in a movie or on TV who is worth giving myself up for. Besides God supplies all my needs according to His riches in glory by Christ Jesus, the anointed One and His anointing.* So as long as he could take care of his end of the bargain, unlike her materialistic sisters, she could handle it. Share and share alike she always said. *And what ever happened to that girl I saw him with that first day? I haven't seen her any more and haven't had the nerve to ask him about her. Then there's my number one priority—my kids—and they adore him, and he adores them. Don't know what Taj would have done without him in his life when we first got here, especially with him being so interested in football and football practically being Kevin's life. And then there's the vision. I respect teachers and coaches to the utmost. I can get up under a mission like that which inspires and influences our young people to be all they can be. It's a part of the solution. I can get with that. Looking at all of that, it seems like Kevin would make a pretty good husband. Wonder what kind of wife I would make with all my baggage? That's for him to determine.*

Niki called Kevin. "We need to talk."

"Be right up."

The kids were outside playing with their friends. They sat at the dining room table, Kevin at the head, Niki across from him. "So what do you have in mind?" Niki asked. Kevin thought *OPPORTUNITY!* Obviously she hadn't dismissed the notion altogether and this was his chance to convince her that the idea wasn't as ridiculous as it may have first seemed.

"I have never felt the way you make me feel. You are smart, funny, open, honest, caring, giving, and absolutely beautiful inside and out. You make me think and laugh. When I'm tired, you inspire me to go on and do what I got to do. You understand me, and I feel your love for me. That feeds my love for you which feeds your love for me, and our love is just growing and growing out of control, and now we have to do something about it." Niki didn't expect all of this. She was speechless. She just sat there and listened. Kevin went on, "I know you've 'been there, done that,' but you said yourself that you no longer want your marriage, haven't been in love with your husband for quite some time, and you need to move on. I know you are waiting to hear from God on that matter, but I have faith that He will give you the go ahead to get out. Have you heard anything from God concerning your marriage yet?" he asked.

Feeling numb, Niki said, "My final decree should be here any day now."

Kevin sat back shocked. *Wow!* He was convinced now more than ever that this relationship was meant to be, and he had to convince her. "Niki, baby, I know that when you get completely divorced, you will move on. I want us to move on together." She was quietly listening to every word. He continued. "Now you have told me about your brothers in the church, and I've seen a couple of them pick you up. You even mentioned about being a damsel in distress, and they take care of you, change your oil, buy you lunch, y'all hang out. I know I got to come with something to put on the table if I expect you to take me seriously. It's not that I don't want you to see other men. Well, that too, but that's not my motivation. You haven't even shown that you are interested in a relationship that way with anybody, and that may have something to do with the way I feel about you. But I know for a fact that in addition to everything else we have, I just want to hold you." There. He said it.

You go, boy. Look at her, she's breaking. You hit it, now drive it home, this might be the only opportunity you have to bring it on home. She might think you're a lunatic and run like crazy. So let everything that comes up come out. This might be your last chance, so go for it. "Niki, baby, I want to hold you like a man holds the woman he loves. I know that it's going to cost me, and I've thought it over and over and I'm willing to pay whatever it takes. Now you know my situation, and I know it's a lot to ask of you with me trying to get established in my career. But, baby, whatever I don't have in finances I'm willing to make up for it in other ways until the finances come, and they *will* come. I'm willing to do whatever, 'cause you are worth it," Kevin pledged. Knowing this serious woman would accept nothing less than a serious offer, he got down on one knee. "Niki, I love you very much. Will you marry me?"

Stunned, Niki asked, "How we gonna do that?"

A cool, confident Kevin said, "Well, we won't say anything to anybody until you receive your final decree, and you are really and truly free. Do the kids know about the divorce?" he asked.

"Yes. When I told them that their daddy and I were not getting back together, they said, 'We kinda figured that out a long time ago, Ma.' Seems I'm
always the last to know stuff. They even said I would probably end up marrying
you. Now ain't that a trip?"

"I always did have a good feeling about those kids. So will you, Niki? I
know you love me. Now go ahead and say it," he said.

"What's love got to do with it?" asked Niki.

"Excellent. Now let me ask you this," he said. "Do you have faith in the
spirit that lives in me?"

Now that was a horse of a different color.

"Yes."

"So, will you marry me?"

"Yes."

CHAPTER 23

Niki hadn't said anything to anybody about the proposal. She was waiting for an assurance of some kind. A sign to fall out of the sky. Kevin didn't ask her anymore. Days went by. Then her final decree came in the mail. *Okay, okay.* Now she could think a little bit. She went downstairs and knocked. Kevin opened the door. She handed him the envelope. He opened it. He read it. Without a word he grabbed her around the waist. She threw her arms around his neck. He lifted her up and spun her around. They laughed. Then he put her down. He took her face in his hands and looked deep into her eyes, the most beautiful eyes he had ever seen. Then he kissed her, ever so gently on the lips. Her knees buckled. He was holding her up. After what seemed like an eternity, they stopped. He looked at her. Tears were in her eyes.

He whispered softly in her ear, "Everything is going to be all right."

She grabbed him tighter. He held her tighter. She couldn't let go. She was exhaling.

Finally she looked into his handsome face and said, "I love you, too. We'll talk later."

Then she left. She had caught him off guard. He had to take a cold shower. He had to make sure he was never caught like that again.

Later Kevin went up to Niki's apartment.

"Have you told the kids?" he asked her.

"No, I was waiting for you," she said.

"Good, let's do this together," he said.

They gathered the kids together. They all sat on the sofa. Holding Niki's hand, which did not go unnoticed by any of the children, Kevin began.

"Your mother and I are best friends. I first realized that I loved her a while back. Now we both realize that we love each other and…"

Miss Mia Hollywood jumped up.

"They're getting married! I'm moving back to Fulton with my daddy!" she yelled.

Niki thought, *This is not going to be easy.* But she let Kevin handle it just to see him under pressure.

"I understand how you feel, Mia. And I will never try to replace your daddy. I love you guys, but it's your mother I want to spend the rest of my life with. We can hang out like we always do. I'll always be here for you, but it's your mother who I want to make happy. She believes I can make her happy. She deserves some happiness, don't you think?"

"Yeah, okay," said Mia and she went into her room to watch TV.

"Here, Taj," Maya said, handing him a dollar.

"Thank you very much," he said, smiling as he took his winnings.

"What's that for?" asked Niki.

"Taj bet me that you two were gonna get married. I said Mommy likes being in control too much, I bet they don't. Thanks a lot, Mommy," Maya said.

"Well, what if I give you your dollar back?" said Niki.

"That'll work," said Maya.

"Are we all still cool?" asked Kevin.

"I'm cool," said Taj.

"Yes, you are, sweetheart," said Niki. "What about my girls?"

"I'm fine, and I know that your little drama queen is, too," said Maya.

Mia was in her room watching TV, going on with her life like nothing even happened.

"Are we still going to the amusement park tomorrow?" asked Taj.

"Just like we planned," said Kevin.

"You coming, Mommy?" asked Maya.

"No, baby, I have some business to take care of."

"I got the kids. You handle your business, baby," said Kevin.

She planned to do just that.

Niki called Jada. "Jada, we have to have a meeting after service tomorrow. Let's get together for brunch."

"Cool. You want me to meet you in the lobby after service?" asked Jada.

"That'll work."

Next, she called Erica. "What's going on after church?"

"Nothing, why?" asked Erica.

"We're meeting for brunch."

"If they got grits, I'll be there."

"Meet Jada and me in the lobby after service."

"Yes, ma'am."

After church service, as they all walked to the car, Erica asked, "Where're the kids, Niki?"

"Kevin is taking them to the amusement park after late service," she responded.

113

"Change his name to State Farm," said Jada.

Erica and Jada sang, "Just like a good ne-ighbooooorr, Sta…"

"Oh, hush up!" Niki interrupted.

They both cracked up.

Niki wanted them in a public place so they wouldn't go off on her when she told them what she had to tell them, and so she wouldn't go off on them if they tried to dis' her man.

At the restaurant they had a beautiful buffet spread from which to choose breakfast dishes, fruit and vegetable salads, all types of seafood, carved beef, and roasted chicken. Niki checked out Erica's plate and shook her head.

"You can take the girl out the country, but you can't take the country out the girl. Is there anything you don't eat grits with, Erica? Smoked salmon, mussels, oysters, poached egg, steamed shrimp, and a bowl of grits," said Niki.

"I can't help it," Erica said, putting a spoonful in her mouth. "Hmmm, they good, too. What is this meeting about?"

"Why didn't you send an interoffice memo so that we could be prepared?" asked Jada.

Erica and Jada laughed. Niki was serious.

"Ladies, I have an announcement to make. Kevin has asked me to marry him, and I have accepted."

She held her breath. Silence. She wondered who would respond first. Erica had the quickest wit today. You never could tell who it would be.

"What, he struck gold since the last time we talked?" said Erica.

Niki decided a new approach. She would just go with the flow.

"Yes. Me," she responded.

"Well, that will be me coughing uncontrollably when the minister asks if anyone here has objections to this union," said Jada.

"You better bring some cough drops," said Niki.

To nip this little exchange and get on with the business at hand, she continued, "See, y'all just mad 'cause I'm going to be getting some and y'all ain't. Now if you don't get off my case, I'm going to call you every day and describe in detail what me and my fine, handsome hunk did the night before. And if you don't answer the phone, I will leave a detailed message on your answering machine."

They both went deadly silent, eyes wide, mouths open, Erica's tongue slightly hanging out.

"Now that I have your attention, understand this. My mama ain't raise no fool. I know when to hold 'em. I know when to fold 'em. I know when to walk away and I sho' nuff know when to run. That's how I got here, how we all got here," Niki continued.

"We know, girl. We're just making sure that you're sure," said Erica.

Jada added, "'Cause if we could shake you, then you need to think about it some more. But you handling your business."

Erica and Jada looked at each other.

"We're going to be bridesmaids," they said, hugging each other.

"Forget the hoopla. We are just going to do it quickly and quietly. Only the people in our Holy of Holies will be there. That's y'all and the kids for me. Randy, Kevin's sister, and her son for him. My folks will do better if I tell them after the fact. That's it. Don't want no spirits I'm not sure about lingering around. Know what I mean? "

"Yeah, girl, we know exactly what you mean," said Erica.

Kevin and Taj went house hunting just about every evening. When they found something that Niki might like, they took her to see it. She didn't like anything. She just wanted something new, fresh, unused and ready to just start living in. There was a new subdivision going up a few blocks away, so they considered building. They fell in love with one particular floor plan, and Niki was ready to sign a contract.

Now it was no secret that Kevin's credit had yet to be established. Niki didn't want to risk not being approved for the loan, therefore she applied alone and was approved almost immediately. The favor of God. The building was begun. It was scheduled to be completed two weeks after her lease was up. Erica invited her to stay with her until it was completed. Two weeks was no big deal, and the kids would be in Virginia for the summer. So she moved in with Erica.

Catching her breath one day, Niki thought, *When things get moving, they move fast!*

Kevin missed Niki not being upstairs and showed up at Erica's sometimes unannounced.

"Look, baby, you can't be coming to this woman's house unannounced," Niki admonished Kevin.

"I know, but when I call, nobody answers or whoever is on the phone ignores the beep 'cause I know you're here. I just want to see my woman," Kevin said.

"We got to follow the house rules," instructed Niki.

"I miss you," he said.

"You see and talk to me every day."

"It's not the same."

They sat on the porch and courted like school kids. It was really sweet to Niki.

"I feel like Erica is your mother and is looking out of the window at us. I know she doesn't want you to marry me. Her or Jada," revealed Kevin.

"Erica is not my mother, okay? Her and Jada are my sisters and they want nothing but the best for me. I'm always totally honest with you, right?" she asked.

"Right," he answered.

"They will only marry men with money and don't feel I should settle. I told them, not that I'm looking for a million dollars or anything, but because you don't have a million dollars today, doesn't mean you won't have a million dollars next year, next month, next week, hey, tomorrow, who knows? God is an awesome God," said Niki

"That's why I love you. You got the faith," said Kevin.

"That's right. I got the faith."

Erica rode to work with Niki.

"He's a little clingy, isn't he?" Erica asked.

"That's all right. As long as he's clinging to me and nobody else." But Niki did value her space, and a seed of doubt was planted.

That same day, the sisters went out for lunch.

"Did you see that dozen, long stem roses that Erica got?" asked Jada. "See that's what my man is going to have to do on a regular basis."

"What's up with Mark? Or is it Lamar? Who is on first this week, Jada?" asked Niki.

"Lamar is out, remember, although he did do the roses thing," she answered.

Niki wondered if the thought ever entered Kevin's mind to send her a dozen long stem roses for no reason at all.

"So who are the roses from, Erica?" asked Jada.

"A preacher who has expressed interest. Got money, too."

"Girl, you can be a preacher's wife?" asked Niki.

"In a heartbeat," said Erica.

"Yeah, I guess you could. You got people skills. I can't even fathom having to deal with all of those personalities and issues," said Niki.

"Oh, I love people. I feel for them. Want to reach out to hurting people and just hug them, just be in a position to bless them all the time," said Erica.

"And I thank God for people like you. Just give me my numbers and let me work them, and I'll tell you what you been doing, how you've been doing, how you can do it better, and what you can expect if you continue to do it that way. People talk back and so do numbers. But you can't argue with numbers. No subjective opinions to deal with. For example, you will never have to waste time debating over the value of a nickel: "I think a nickel should be worth six cents." "Well I think it should be worth four." A nickel is worth five cents no matter what anybody thinks. End of discussion. Just give me my numbers."

"I believe balance is the key to life," said Jada. "Every now and then, I have to stop working for money. I mean my profession is so cutthroat, to make sure I don't get caught up in it, I periodically get out of the rat race and give back, I mean just sow. I'm in that mode now."

"She has great organization skills, and we are blessed to have her volunteering at the ministry," said Erica. "Jada, if you ever decide not to go back, consider coming on board here at the church."

"No way. I need to be free to do what I got to do, when I got to do it," said Jada.

"Amen," said Niki. "I have things to do, too, that I don't need to be jumping through no hoops to get done. It's good you are taking that into consideration, Jada. I didn't take that or the money into consideration when I accepted the position. But I got to be honest with y'all. Ecclesiastes says there's a time for everything. And I no longer believe that this position is where I am to be until Jesus comes like I did when I first got it. I really believed I had arrived. But I can see now that once I have accomplished what God called me here to do, He might move me on. Especially if y'all don't get that money right, Erica. I'm building a house and I ain't depending on no man to meet my needs. Especially when I am qualified to meet my own. And that's all I got to say about that."

"I hear you, girl. Pastor told us in staff meeting that if the ministry is not meeting your needs, get to where you can get your needs met," said Erica.

"That he did, and that's what opened my eyes," said Niki.

"So hey, we'll just continue to flow. But I still need a man who can pay all my bills," said Erica.

Even though Niki had convinced herself that she didn't need a man to take care of her, she thought about what Erica said.

Kevin picked Niki up and they went to check on the house. Niki had been really quiet lately, deep in thought. Kevin didn't feel comfortable with the way she was acting. He felt her pulling away. He didn't know what to do. There was nothing he could do.

"How was your day?" he asked.

"Fine," was all she said.

They went to the movies. Niki hardly laughed at all, and the movie was hilarious. Something was clearly on her mind. She was having second thoughts.

"Talk to me, sweetheart," he said.

Don't sweet talk me like that. It makes it difficult for me to say what I got to say, she thought. "Kevin, I am 37 years old. I have been married and divorced. I have three highly active, very intelligent children. I am well established in my career and I need stability. You are 27 years old, no children, never been married, are doing substitute teaching, and are enrolled in school. The kids and I are used to certain things. Now there's a house and all the responsibility that comes along with it," said Niki.

"What's your point, Niki?" Kevin asked.

"In your current position, we're a lot for you to take on all at once. You stand a better chance of making it alone, because I don't think you have taken into consideration everything that you are getting into. As for me, I didn't come to Zion to get married. I haven't been free in a long time. I need to be by myself, to get to know myself all over again as the woman I have become with everything I have been through. God will meet my needs. I don't think we should do this. We should just not see each other anymore to make it easier. I'll get the house and believe God to provide."

Kevin was devastated. "It's those girlfriends of yours. Sisters Super Christians. They need to mind their own business. Where are their husbands? They don't have any, and they don't want you to have one either. I can't believe you are falling for that garbage," he shouted in anger. "Y'all women are a trip. I thought you were different, Niki. But if you want to be like them and live in La La Land waiting for a Prince Charming to ride in on a white horse and take you to the palace and live happily ever after, then trip on. I just wanted to love you. You know we can do this. You know it, Niki. I don't believe this."

He left her sitting on the porch, heart breaking from having hurt him. He got in the car.

"I just don't freakin' believe this bull," he said as he sped off.

Niki sat on the porch and cried for an hour.

Kevin was angry, angrier than he had been in a long, long time. How could he be this upset over a woman except that it was the real thing? The way he was feeling, he knew he couldn't let anything come between them. He had to calm down and think. *Lord, don't let me lose her. Don't let those so called "sisters" of hers influence her to turn away from me. Make her see that we can do this. You put this feeling in me and in her because neither one of us had any intention of this happening. You got to make it work, Lord. Show us how to make it work. Amen.*

That night Niki told Erica the marriage was off.

"Are you sure?" Erica asked.

"Yeah," responded Niki. "It's for the best."

Erica was not convinced.

The next day, Kevin called Niki.

"Hello, sweetheart," he said.

118

"Hi, Kevin," she said.

"I apologize for losing it," he said.

"I didn't mean to upset you. I meant what I said, but God knows I don't want to hurt you," Niki said, confused and torn between doing what her heart versus her head said to do.

"I heard what you said and I understand your point, but I think we need to talk it through. Would you please have dinner with me tomorrow? I will fix something special for you."

Niki didn't know if he could cook or not. This might be interesting.

"Okay," she said.

Kevin picked Niki up after work, and they went to his apartment. Randy was out for the evening. He set the table complete with candles and borrowed wine glasses for the chilled sparkling apple cider. He sat her down at the table and brought in mixed-matched plates with collard greens, corn, and bourbon chicken over rice. It looked delicious. He certainly knew what she liked. Nothing elegant, but real food that tasted real good. And it did. It was absolutely delicious.

"You threw down, Kevin, I had no idea you could cook like this," complimented Niki.

Kevin just chewed and smiled.

Niki thought, *How polite, he doesn't want to talk with his mouth full.*

After they ate and were going to the sofa to talk, Niki stopped in the kitchen to pour herself some more cider. She spotted the take-out boxes in the trash can. She glanced around the kitchen and didn't see a dirty dish except their plates. No pots, no pans, no bowls of food. What if she wanted some more to eat, what would he say? She was tempted to ask for seconds, but thought, *If we weren't going to have this serious talk I'd mess with him about this wonderful meal he supposedly cooked.* She thought he was absolutely adorable, resisted the urge to call him Mrs. Doubtfire and let it go.

As they sat on the sofa and sipped cider by candlelight, he put his arm around her and she leaned back against him.

"How do you feel?" he asked.

"Wonderful," she answered.

"Good," he said.

Both of them were feeling things they had never felt before.

"Niki, you shocked me yesterday, baby. That's no excuse for going off like I did, but what we have is so real I can't believe you would let somebody come between us."

"It's not somebody, Kevin. There already is a gap between us—age and experiences, that I don't know if you have really sat down and considered."

119

"I've considered everything I could think of, everything that we have talked about, and I have especially considered my feelings for you. You don't feel it, too?" he asked.

"I do, but there is so much more to consider," she said.

"I thought the Bible said love conquers all," he said.

"It does."

"Then why do we have to keep considering?"

While she tried to think of a logical response, he took her face and gently kissed her lips. So much for her coming up with a logical response. She responded, but not in words. She turned towards him and kissed him back. As they kissed, Niki's spirit was sending out warning signals all over the place. Alarms were ringing inside her head so loud that they almost gave her a headache, yet she was helpless to do anything about it. The still, small voice that she had come to know in such an intimate way was drowned out by the sirens.

She had no strength whatsoever to stop Kevin from picking her up and taking her into his bedroom. Her mind escaped to oblivion as her flesh overtook her spirit. Every part of her womanhood was awakened from a deep, deep sleep to help her flesh defeat her spirit as he kissed and caressed her body. Her spirit was trying to fight back, but it all felt so natural, so wonderful, so perfect that she had no desire to stop. A serious battle was being waged between her spirit and her flesh. But it was all in vain. When her emotions kicked in, her mind checked out. Kevin's touches sent her mind running for cover because it had sense enough not to stick around and be held responsible for what was about to happen; therefore, her spirit could not find her will to say stop. She would not be able to logically defend what was about to happen because her intellect, like her will, ran with her mind. Thus, the battle was over; her flesh had won and she surrendered as they made the sweetest, most passionate love either one of them had ever experienced. They slept all night in each other's arms.

The next morning as she was entering the house, Erica greeted her at the door.

"Where have you been, like I don't know?" asked Erica.

Niki said nothing, didn't look at her, and kept walking to her room and closed the door.

"Girl, that is some dangerous ground," Erica threw in before she realized this was a subject Niki was not opening up for discussion. At that point, she made the quick decision to never bring it up again, but just be there for Niki if she ever wanted to talk about it and to pray for her sister's strength.

As absolutely beautiful as it was, Niki felt as worthless as a penny with a hole in it. She didn't say anything to anybody. Everyone thought she was either sick or real busy and didn't bother her. They knew how intense she was about her work and pretty much left her alone, for which she was grateful.

Kevin called. Unfortunately for him her mind had come out of hiding.

"Never, ever, do I want to see you again. You made me sin against my Father, against my Lord and Savior Jesus, against everything I believe in. I grieved the Holy Spirit. I profess to be this big time, spiritually deep, super Christian and I am nothing but a fornicator. And so are you. Like I said the other day, it is best that we end this right now. Goodbye for real this time, Kevin, and I mean it," she said and hung up the phone with a definite finality.

Kevin was on the other end holding a dead phone, shaking his head. *I knew it, I just knew it,* he thought. *It was just too beautiful, too perfect.* He had found his soul mate and lost her just because he loved her.

"Lord, how could something so beautiful be so wrong? You got to show me. I see that it's best if I give her some time to seek You on this as I need to seek You for myself. Give me the strength to stay away from her. In Jesus' name, Amen."

CHAPTER 24

She was depressed, down, and quiet. If her children were there, they would surely know that something was wrong. They always knew when something was wrong with her, so she thanked God they weren't there because she wouldn't be able to face them. It probably wouldn't have happened had her children been there. She realized that her children were an added incentive for her to live a righteous and holy life. Being their example of faith in action gave her strength to "Just Say No" to temptation. But they weren't there to save her from herself. She had fallen, and without them there, it didn't seem that she could get up.

She went to work, came home, and went to bed every day for a week. The house still wasn't ready. The builders had requested another extension so her time was prolonged at Erica's, which was fine with Erica. She was so busy that she didn't even notice Niki was there most of the time. Nor did she notice her depressed state.

Niki hadn't said one word to God since she and Kevin made love. She felt unworthy to even ask for forgiveness. She just laid in the bed every day after work. She cried that she had let God down after all He had done for her. She was supposed to be setting this godly example for Kevin and ended up causing him to sin and then blamed him for causing her to sin. She didn't even take responsibility for her own actions, which is what she had always gotten on Rae about.

She began to listen to tapes on forgiveness and let the Word of God minister to her as she laid in bed. Eventually she felt that God knew how sorry she was. As she laid in bed she felt the love of God engulfing her, forgiving her, cleansing her. She felt peace overcome her. She remembered Jesus hanging on the cross and shedding His blood for her sins so that she didn't have to do what she was doing, and she began to feel joy again.

Joy unspeakable suddenly overcame her, and she jumped up and shouted "Hallelujah! Glory to God! Praise You, Jesus! Father, I have sinned against You in the form of fornication, and according to 1 John 1:9 You said if we confess our sins, You are faithful and just to forgive us our sins and to cleanse us from all unrighteousness. I believe Your Word, Lord, and I receive Your forgiveness, and if You can forgive me, then I can forgive myself. Hallelujah!" she prayed.

She knew it was over between her and Kevin and that she had to get on with her life. It was for the best. He had his whole life ahead of him. She had lived one life and was in the middle of her next one. She hadn't had a lot of time to think about what she wanted to do with the rest of her life, and because her relationship with Kevin "just happened" she didn't feel she was in on the planning and decision making process. That was a part of Niki's controlling nature, wanting to be in on everything because she honestly believed that her input was valuable. She knew she had to cut Kevin completely off for now. He made it easy for her by staying away. After a couple of weeks had passed, he called her.

"Hello, this is Kevin. I'm calling to see how you're doing."

"I'm fine."

"That's good. That's real good. I know the Lord is taking good care of you. I wish you nothing but the best. You deserve it," he said.

"Thank you; you too."

"Bye now."

"Bye."

The house was finally finished. Niki had been praying for a smooth closing. It went perfect and she got the keys to her new home. She moved in and got everything straight because the kids were due back that weekend.

When they arrived, they ran through the house and praised the Lord for the space to stretch out. They loved their apartment, but the kids had lived in a house all their lives and weren't use to tiptoeing around because neighbors lived under them.

They had a ceremony to dedicate the house to God. They sanctified it and anointed it with oil. They gave God all the honor, praise, and glory for blessing them in such a mighty way. They were confused as to why Kevin wasn't there, but were afraid to ask their mother.

Niki hadn't seen Kevin for over a month. He would call from time to time just to say hi, and she really believed she was over him because she wasn't thinking about him. Sure she was busy picking out lighting, carpet, tile, marble, paint, and every single thing that went into the house, dealing with movers, scheduling the kids' return and everything else a thoroughbred superwoman does. She really hadn't had time to think about Kevin. So when he called this particular time, he caught her off guard.

"Hey, Niki, this is Kevin."

"Hey, Kevin."

"Listen, I was looking in the closet and I found that portable fan that you left in the apartment. I went up there and checked one day for anything you may have left behind and found it. I was holding it for you. I forgot to mention it."

123

"Oh, that's where it is? I was wondering what happened to it."

"I can bring it to you."

"Okay," she said thinking she was completely over him. "What's a good time for you?"

"I'm not busy now," he said.

"Okay, you can bring it on over."

"Be there in a few minutes."

"Thanks, Kev." She said it like she should have added old buddy, old pal, convinced that it was safe to go back to their original friendship. He was the best friend. The kind that you keep forever if you are ever blessed enough to find such a rare, precious one like him. She was excited at the thought of having her old friend back in her life. She looked forward to seeing him.

The doorbell rang. A naive Niki ran to the door and opened it. She gasped for breath at the sight of him. He smiled the most beautiful smile in the world.

"Hello, Sister Niki," he said.

She opened her mouth, but nothing came out. He was literally glowing. He had lost weight and was tight as a drum. He was taller, straighter, and strength exuded from him. He had on a T-shirt and his biceps looked like brown hard balls. He looked like he had just gotten out of the barber's chair, and his beard was perfectly trimmed. He smelled wonderful, and Niki was subconsciously taking deep breaths trying to inhale him. Every womanly instinct she had was screaming *Grab him, grab him.* She leaned towards him, and he responded by putting the fan down and hugging her. It was only slightly more than a friendly hug, the efforts on both their parts keeping it in check.

Niki, in her trademark honesty, said, "I don't know what you have been doing, Brother, but you need to keep on doing it. Come on in and talk to me."

He followed her in the house and looked around.

"This is absolutely beautiful, baby, I mean Sister Niki."

"Thanks."

She gave him the grand tour.

"Now tell me, what have you been doing?" she asked.

"Well, let me see. I tried something you said that you did that was real powerful. I started going to the throne first thing every morning."

"I knew I recognized that glow," she interjected.

"It was probably your glow that attracted me to you in the first place," he said.

"Hey, you cannot spend time with God and the glory doesn't get on you. People can see it, too. Look at you. I knew you had been in the presence of God. I just knew it. Go on," she said, thrilled that he had found his way to the throne.

"Well, in addition to regularly attending church, I have been going to a Bible study at a frat brother's place in Payten County, and that's been a blessing."

"Was that the guy I saw with you at church Sunday?" she asked.

"Probably, because he did go with me. The Bible is so awesome. My eyes have really been opened." He hesitated before he made his next statement. "Then I changed careers."

Niki looked shocked. "What?"

"Yeah, I decided to use what I already had, my business degree, and get a corporate job. On that fast track to management, great salary, great benefits. Everything I need to take care of a family."

Niki didn't know what to think.

"Since when?" she asked.

"A couple of weeks," he said.

"How's it going?" she asked. knowing what the corporate world was like and wondering how a man like Kevin fit in.

"Pretty good. It's not the classroom, but it's a living. How's it going with you?" he asked.

"I got one more trip this year. Just still in awe of the impact we're making on the world. But with all of that, I definitely have to reconsider some things. The house makes a difference. Can't just call somebody to come fix stuff anymore like in the apartment," she said.

"You can call me, and if I was here, you wouldn't even have to do that," he said.

Stop it, I said, Niki thought.

Kevin figured now that Niki was in her own place and away from the influences of her super manless Christian sisters that he might have another chance. He couldn't even think of another woman the whole time he was away from her. Even when Randy insisted he get somebody to help him forget Niki, he went to God instead.

"I still love you, Niki. I always will. You mean everything to me. It's hell not being with you. The only thing that gets me through is going to the throne. God made it all right. If I work hard, I can move on up that corporate ladder, and we can have the life you deserve, baby."

"Kevin, we can't just ignore what happened. I was supposed to be setting a godly example before you and look what happened," Niki said, unaware that she was still stuck in guilt trip mode.

Kevin was confused. Didn't she know she was a woman even before she was a Christian? *Why, when folks get saved, do they try to stop being real?* he wondered. "I know you are a Christian and so am I. I know what the Bible says about what we should and should not do and we most definitely were wrong. I have asked for forgiveness, and I know you have, too, and it's over. But I'm confused about why you are still beating yourself up for what happened. Look at you. You are a real, warm, sensuous, flesh and blood woman, to the bone, baby, and what happened was perfectly natural. I'm not justifying what happened because we should not have let it get to that point. We should have gone out to eat or something. But once it got past a certain point, there was nothing either one of us could have done to stop the inevitable. Don't fool yourself that because you are so spiritually deep that you can handle anything. None of us can. Lack of vision and thinking we would never do such a thing against God was the trap that we both fell into. Paul told us that in the flesh dwells no good thing. I thought we would be okay too, because we had some serious issues to discuss. Never did I think for one second that that would happen, but it did. It wasn't planned, it wasn't premeditated. What it was, was confirmation that you are supposed to be my wife. How long can we deny this love? It is too strong, too real, and you have got to come out of denial about that."

She knew he was right. She was supposed to be the mature Christian and he the baby Christian, and here he had sought the Lord, gotten understanding, received his forgiveness, and gone on with his life while she was walking around depressed and in denial about her womanhood. He was ready. She was ready.

"When do you want to begin premarriage counseling?" she asked.

"Immediately," he answered.

CHAPTER 25

Erica and Jada were not surprised when Niki told them that the marriage was back on. They knew that she really loved Kevin and that he really loved her. They were truly happy for her.

After Niki and Kevin completed marriage counseling, they decided to hold the ceremony right away. Neither one of them wanted to wait any longer to be together than they had to. It just appeared that too many forces were working to keep them apart and united they would be a stronger force to reckon with.

Erica and Jada set up the honeymoon suite at a swank hotel because they knew that their basic, let's-just-get-this-done, one-track-minded, don't-spend-no-money-on-no-one-day-when-we-need-stuff-for-the-house thinking sister hadn't given it much thought.

"Thank you so much, 'cause we had already decided that our new bedroom in our new house in our new king size bed would have been honeymoon suite enough," said Niki.

"Girl, you are so tired," said Erica. "I am bringing a respirator on my honeymoon in case my husband needs more oxygen, because I do plan to work him."

"Thanks and we do appreciate you," Niki said.

The ceremony was so special. The glory of God filled the room. Every spirit was in agreement. It was so intimate, so close and so personal that all who were present knew that this union was clearly ordered by God. The bond that was formed that day could never ever be broken by anything or anyone other than the groom or his bride.

"I now pronounce you man and wife. You may now salute your bride," said the minister.

After Kevin saluted his bride, he breathed easier. Niki had breathed easier when she didn't hear any coughing during the entire ceremony.

Erica took the kids home with her as the bride and groom left for the honeymoon suite. Kevin scooped Niki up and carried her across the threshold. He sat her on his lap and looked up at her. She was looking at him, smiling. All the love they had been carrying for each other was about to, on purpose, get unleashed, and right now he had to go to the bathroom.

Niki poured the sparkling apple cider into the long stemmed crystal glasses marked bride and groom and thought, *Thanks, Jada.* She looked in the drawer, as Erica had instructed her, and there was a beautiful white lace teddy that had Erica written all over it. It was elegant and Niki put it on. She looked beautiful. Then she put on Kevin's jacket to surprise him.

When he came out of the bathroom with tie hanging, shirt open, he looked at Niki sitting in the chair with his jacket on, handing him a glass. When he walked over to her to get it, she opened the jacket and he stopped suddenly in his tracks. He took his time absorbing this vision of beauty making sure it was branded in his mind so that he could come back to it at anytime. His eyes having sufficiently feasted, he got down on his knees in front of Niki.

He took the glass and they toasted, "To God," he said and they touched glasses and sipped.

"To love," she said and they touched glasses again and sipped.

Together they said "To us," and wrapped arms and sipped.

He put his glass on the night table by the bed. He took her glass and put it beside his. He gently kissed her forehead, her cheeks, her neck, her shoulders. She was in flames. He had purposed in his heart to make her forget every negative thing, every hurt, every pain, every disappointment, and every fear she had ever dealt with, at least for this night.

When the honeymooners got home, all was well. The kids were excited to have a man in the house, especially since it was Kevin who they had no doubt loved their mother very much.

Kevin and Taj moved Kevin's things into the garage. Kevin was the complete opposite of Niki—he only had what he needed, which wasn't much, and for that, Niki was grateful. They were able to mingle their things together with no problems. The adjustment was smooth as silk for no other reason than this union was truly meant to be.

When Niki went to work and informed everybody that she was married, she got mixed reactions. None of them mattered. She was basking in the glory of God. Questions were being asked, things were being said, little comments were being made. Niki had made a decision to be oblivious to it all.

"Let me know when you get done tripping off my life," she would say and laugh.

She had a special knack for separating that which mattered from that which did not matter. If it wasn't a kingdom issue, Niki could not be bothered. A term she liked to use was "insignificant." If someone said something off the wall to her she would say, "There is no time in my life allotted for such insignificant matters." The comments eventually subsided, and it was work as usual.

Kevin had been having challenges from day one on his job. The corporate environment was just not him. He missed the classroom so much he could hardly stand it. Niki was raised in corporate America. She had corporate skills and could handle herself. Kevin was young, naive, inexperienced, and just too honest for corporate America. He did his best, which wasn't quite good enough because his heart just wasn't in it. This was a man who followed his heart to Niki, but now wondered if giving up his career goals to get her was the right thing to do. He was not happy, and it began to affect his work. Eventually it affected his homelife. He was despondent and withdrawn from second guessing his decision. If Niki couldn't accept him where he was, should he be with her? Why should he give up his dreams? Why didn't she have a little more patience? He would go talk to Randy and the people from the Bible study about things in general. He prayed, but he was still pulling away from Niki because subconsciously he blamed her for getting him off track with his career goals, although it was his decision. He truly thought that this was the best thing to do at the time. He had figured that being with the woman he loved was going to make everything all right. Maybe he was being naive. Love can't make you happy on a job you hate. Finally he got the desire of his heart. He got fired. He felt relief he hadn't felt in a long time, but knew that it would be short lived when he told his wife.

"Fired! Only fools get fired." She couldn't imagine being married to an unemployed man. That went against everything she ever believed. That meant she had to take care of him on her church salary, and she panicked at the thought.

"Baby, I can still go back to the classroom," which is all he ever wanted to do anyway. "You won't have to take care of me. I will get a part time job and we'll be fine."

Unstable, unstable, unstable is all that rang in Niki's ears. *Even marriage counseling doesn't prepare you that well for the way the world works these days, everything being so flip flopped,* she thought.

"It's not supposed to be like this; I'm a rock and you're a weeble wobble. It's supposed to be the other way around," she screamed.

Fear had opened the door for the devil to get in, and he took advantage of the opportunity. Because Niki wasn't being her sweet understanding self, and Kevin was under pressure outside the home, he was finding it more and more difficult to deal with the pressures inside the home. Every day Niki wanted to know where he was on the job situation. He couldn't even stand talking to her anymore because it was more like an interrogation. One evening she was trying to talk to him, and he just got up and walked away.

"Don't you walk away from me when I'm talking to you," Niki said as she ran and jumped on his back.

Instinctively he twisted her off his back, picked her up, and threw her on the sofa just as Maya came out of her room and witnessed the whole thing.

129

"Leave my mother alone!" she screamed.

Niki, unhurt from landing on the soft sofa, was instantly sorry for what she had done in front of her daughter and knew that some changes had to be made.

Kevin knew from the look on Maya's face that he had to leave. He was overwhelmed. He hadn't bargained for all of this. He didn't know what to say. He had to go think, go pray.

"I'm outta here," he said.

And he left.

Niki held Maya, who was crying.

"Shhhh, everything will be all right, baby. He didn't hurt me. He could never hurt me."

CHAPTER 26

"Neither one of them! Not one of them. Not the book and not the movie. Nothing showed what happened after that older woman married that young boy. That's messed up setting us up to think this mess is all peaches and cream. BULL! She needs to write the sequel and tell us just how long her groove lasted after she married him. That's what I want to know," Niki vented.

Jada and Erica let her vent as they ate popcorn, ice cream and cake, and drank lemonade in the middle of Erica's living room floor.

"If I missed God on this one, I don't want to see no man. Superman Prince Charming Denzel Dash-Rip-Rock-afeller better not approach me," yelled Niki.

"I can't believe you jumped on his back. What were you going to do, beat the big 220 pound linebacker up?" asked Jada.

"I'll tell you what it was," said Erica. "That was the harvest from the seed she planted talking about my grits. Talking about you can take the girl out the country, but you can't take the country out the girl 'cause I love my grits. Well, you, my sweet loving sister in Christ, love to fight. And you can take the girl out the hood, but you can't take the hood out the girl. You need to be delivered from outta there."

"Ouch! But you're right. I want to slam me one right about now. Think the champ will let me work out in his gym? Just let me, I said let me now, beat up on some of his sparing partners. Ask him for me, Erica," said Niki.

"Lord, help her," said Erica.

"I hope I'm not affecting your decision to marry Mark, Jada."

"Not at all, girl. Mark and I have built a successful law practice together, and I have seen every side of him. And believe me, money brings out the worst in people. We love each other, our trust has been reestablished, and we are going to do this. There is nothing you can do to change my mind. So rant and rave on. Get it off your chest, knock yourself completely out, because my wedding is on," said Jada.

"You need to go home and work it out with your husband. That man worships the ground you walk on. I wish a man felt like that about me. Ain't nothing God can't handle," Erica said.

"Yeah, get him back in that house as soon as possible," said Jada.

"Can't do that. That violent demon I thought was long gone jumped up on me before I knew it, and I got to make sure that sucker is gone before I subject my kids to that foolishness. It's not him; it's me. I need some time," said Niki.

"I know he and Randy are boys, but it's not good for a married man to be living with a single man. He's beyond that. He can't go back there. Too many temptations. Too many memories. Get your man back in the house with you," commanded Jada.

"We got a lot of talking to do first. He sacrificed his goals to marry me, and I was so blinded by love I missed the fact that he was sabotaging his career for me. I was being so selfish that I allowed him to give up that part of him that I love the most, his vision to help boys like himself to succeed in life. Oh, God, I am such an evil, no good, selfish, lowdown, dirty person, unworthy of a man like Kevin," Niki cried out, falling on the floor.

"Now I see where Mia gets it from. Please give Drama Mama here an academy award," said Jada.

With the revelation that the pity party she was trying to have wasn't going to happen, especially with these party poopers, Niki jumped up. "Okay, okay. What do I need to pray for 'cause we are going to touch and agree for it."

"You need patience," said Erica.

"I need not to be so selfish."

"You need more wisdom and understanding," said Jada.

"You need to bind the devil from your house, your family, and your marriage," said Erica.

"Yeah, yeah. That's right. You got it. All that. Let's pray," said Niki.

They set on the floor in a circle, holding hands, touching and agreeing as one. Niki prayed. "Father, we come to you in the name of Your Son, Jesus Christ, the anointed One, and His anointing who came to remove our burdens and destroy our yokes. You said in your Word that where two or three are gathered together in My name, there am I in the midst of them. We know You are here, Jesus, seated right here with us. We feel your presence. You are always with us. You said You will never leave us nor forsake us. Even when we mess up You forgive us. You said if any man lacks wisdom let him ask, and You will liberally give it to him. We ask for Your wisdom, Lord. We have the mind of Christ. We bind the enemy according to Matthew 18:18: 'Whatsoever things are bound in earth are bound in heaven.' We bind the enemy from my marriage, our homes, our lives, and our families in the name of Jesus. We quench every fiery dart that the devil has aimed at us with the Word of God that is sharper than any two-edged sword and accomplishes what we send it to accomplish. The Holy Spirit who lives on the inside of us and knows all things, teaches us all things that pertain to life and godliness. We, as women of God, flow in the fruit of the spirit which is love, joy, peace, longsuffering, gentleness, goodness, faith, meekness and temperance. Father, you make the crooked roads straight in our lives. My marriage is crooked right now, Lord, and it's a burden to me. I lay my burdens down at Your feet right now, because You said to cast my cares on You because You care for me. You perfect those things that concern me, and my marriage is a major concern right now. Fix it Lord, as only You can. I am more than a conqueror through Jesus Christ, my Lord and my Savior; therefore, I receive the VICTORY right now in Jesus' name. Amen."

And they all said, "Amen."

Kevin called and invited Niki out to dinner to talk. She agreed.

"Baby, I didn't realize it at the time, but I wasn't being totally honest with myself. I didn't want to put my career on hold. I didn't want to get a corporate job. But most of all, I didn't want to lose you. So I lied to myself and was miserable. I thought I could handle it," he said.

Niki said, "I'm sorry for being so selfish that I didn't realize what you were sacrificing for us to be together. I fell in love with you *because of* your dreams and goals. Even when Pastor preached from the pulpit don't marry potential, I still believed in you. Then when you asked me, after we established that love wasn't enough, if I had faith in you, I knew I did because you had it in yourself to the point where it was contagious."

"Do you have faith and patience enough to work with me to get my career established?" asked Kevin.

"Hmmmm, this feels like deja vu, but I realize I tripped and let fear in. I reneged on the contract, and because of the breach, all heck broke loose," explained Niki.

"I tripped too, baby, and I apologize. I was miserable, but I couldn't risk losing you. I promise to be completely honest with you from now on," said Kevin.

"I promise to be understanding. And we'll figure everything else out," said Niki.

Kevin was silent for a minute, deep in thought. Finally he spoke. "In the heat of battle, some things came out that I had never seen before," he said.

"I know," she said, knowing she had to face it sooner or later.

"Now I love you with all my heart, but under no circumstances will violence be tolerated. I would never put my hands on you," said Kevin.

"I know," said Niki, barely audible.

"At the same time, I'm not going to let you put your hands on me either," he said.

"I know," she said, nodding her head.

"I'll get you off me and leave."

"I know."

133

"That can never, ever, never, ever, ever happen again."

"I know," she said, bobbing her head up and down quickly.

"Nothing, and I mean nothing is worth going through that."

"I totally agree," Niki said, finally thinking of something different to say.

"Maybe we can look into some counseling or some kind of help controlling your temper. I'll help you, baby, because I want to be with you, but not under those circumstances," Kevin said.

"I know," she said, reverting backward. "I'll talk to the counselors at the church.

"Okay, we'll go together," he said.

"Okay." She paused trying to think of anything else they needed to cover. Finally she said, "Well, all the cards are certainly on the table."

"Indeed they are," responded Kevin.

"Oh, I almost forgot. It's truly harvest time. You know that job I was looking into? They made me an offer. It's time for an increase. I accepted it," Niki said beaming.

"Praise the Lord. But are you sure you want to step out of your calling?" asked Kevin.

"I believe I accomplished what I was called to Way Maker Ministries to do. My department runs like a fine-tuned clock, and my assistant is thoroughly trained to do my job. They will be fine. That's God's business, and He will always take care of His business. Now I got to take care of mine and put the sickle to the harvest. It's time. I always say, I know when to hold 'em and I know when to fold 'em. I wanna hold you. Is that okay?"

"You gotta ask?"

"Then, I believe our business is done here."

"Well, let's go home."

Mark and Jada's wedding was the most elegant, intimate wedding the church had ever seen. The wedding party consisted of Niki, Erica, and Mark and Jada's children. All the females had on peach and cream, including the bride. Jada's gown was exquisite. A few clients and associates were invited, but very few.

When the minister asked Jada if she took this man to be her lawfully wedded husband, Jada didn't respond right away. Fear gripped bridesmaids Niki and Erica simultaneously as they both stared directly at Jada's mouth in anticipation of the word "yes" coming out. They couldn't imagine what she was waiting for. The wait seemed like an eternity during which time neither one of them breathed.

Erica thought, *No, no, no. Not now. Please don't back out now. Just say yes; say it Jada, say it.*

Niki was thinking, *Girl, if you are changing your mind, you better lie and say "yes" now and get this over with. You can repent later. God will forgive you for lying. I promise He will. Don't mess this up, 'cause I wouldn't know what to do.*

Finally, Jada said, "Yes, I will."

Niki and Erica both let out a great big sigh of relief, but were nervous wrecks for the rest of the ceremony.

As the bridal party proceeded up the aisle and out the door, Niki grabbed Jada's left arm and Erica grabbed her right arm, and they escorted her into the ladies room, leaving Mark standing there with a confused smile stuck on his face.

"What the heck was that all about?" asked Niki.

Erica was practically in tears. "Girl, my heart is beating so fast I might have to go get it checked. What's up?" she asked.

Jada was crying, and at the exact same moment, Niki and Erica recognized them as tears of joy.

"I have everything I ever wanted. The single struggle is over. You are my best friends, and I love you so much. But it was so hard sometimes I just couldn't even talk about it. I just prayed my way through, and now God has blessed me beyond my greatest expectations and I had to thank Him right then and there," Jada explained.

Both Niki and Erica, relieved, began to cry. Niki, because she knew and understood Jada's struggle and was happy that it was over for her sister friend. Erica cried because she just loved happy endings. They hugged and cried together, rejoicing in the goodness of the Lord. Then they put themselves back together, fixing hair, makeup and gowns to take pictures. The sisters joined the rest of the party, Jada glowing with the radiance of God. All three looked absolutely elegant, like the virtuous women that they were.

The reception was just as intimate, just as elegant as the wedding, with no surprises. The sit down dinner setting and beautiful soft music made for wonderful fellowship. The Alexanders were positioned for explosive growth. God had definitely established this union to funnel the wealth of the wicked into the hands of the just, and quickly. And they were ready to receive it.

CHAPTER 27

Erica had been feeling left out since her sisters had gotten married. Even though they still hung out for dessert and coffee, did movies, brunch, and birthdays, Erica began distancing herself from them. She felt she shouldn't spend that much time with married women, and married women shouldn't spend that much time with single women. She began to spend more time fellowshipping with other single women, although nobody could replace her sisters that she loved so dearly.

One night as she was riding on the interstate thinking about her girlfriends and their husbands and families, she asked God where was her husband. She wanted to be married with a family to satisfy that loving nurturing side of her. She had believed God, she had prayed, she had gone out with potential suitors. Had her husband been there and she missed him being, as Niki said, too picky? She just wanted God's best and didn't want to settle. She began to cry because she was so lonely. She began to cry out to God.

"Why, Lord, why am I not married? Where is my husband? I am ready. I really want someone to love and to love me in the natural."

While she was crying out to God, her car died. It just cut off. She coasted to the side of the road and tried to start it again. Nothing. This was not happening to her. She got out, then thought, *What am I going to do*? The mood she had been in made her not even care about the potential dangers.

"God! Oh, God!" she cried, "Help me!"

She sat on the side of the road and just let it all out. She was crying more about her loneliness than about her car situation.

"I just want to be loved and held and comforted."

She wasn't even concerned about the car now.

"Oh, God, I know You have my husband out there somewhere. Manifest him, Lord! Bring him to me!" she screamed violently, letting everything she had bottled up inside of her out of her. She didn't even notice the headlights shining on her from behind her car. Nor did she see the stranger get out of the back seat and walk up to her.

"Looks like you need some help, sister," said a strong, deep voice.

She looked up startled, but unafraid. From the headlights of a white limo she could see a gorgeous man standing in front of her. Way deep down on the inside of her she heard a still small voice say, "Here is your husband." As she squinted to get a better look, he reached his hand out to her. She gave him her hand.

It was almost exactly one year later that the sisters were putting the finishing touches on their makeup inside the dressing room.

"God is an awesome God. Just look at Him," Erica said in a bridal gown that cost $10,000.

"A year ago, I was sitting on the side of the road in the cold, wailing, crying out to God. Now a year later, Niki's first novel is on the New York Times Bestsellers List, and she got a seven figure advance for the movie rights."

"Heeeyyy!!" said Niki, waving her hands in the air.

Erica continued, "Kevin has been nominated for an Image Award for his work with young black males in the community. His team won the state championship, and all of his senior football players are going to college, thanks to him, 'cause he wouldn't stop pushing, working, talking, looking for funds until they were all in."

"That's my man," said Niki.

"Alexander and Alexander is rapidly gaining a reputation for being a young but powerful and prestigious law firm," said Erica.

"Won't take a case I can't win," said Jada. "We're undefeated in the courtroom because we are more than conquerors. Only take the cases God says to take. Pray over every one to create that win-win situation. Jesus is the real counselor's counsel. And a wonderful One, let me tell you."

"I hear ya, girl. And I am about to marry my Knight In Shining Armor who rode up in his white limo to rescue me off of the side of the road. What's that you say about fairy tales, Niki?" asked Erica, joy overflowing.

"Just believe and you shall receive. I always said that, and you know it, Cinderella!" said Niki, ecstatic for her sister.

The sisters hugged and laughed and praised their Father God Almighty.

It was time. The church was packed with Erica's family and friends, just about everybody who knew her. Richard's congregation packed the rest of the church. He was the son of the pastor of one of the largest churches in the country. He was a minister himself, and the CEO of his father's church. His father had been praying for him to settle down and get married, being a man in his position, but he had been waiting for the perfect bride. He refused to settle. The women in his church had done mind-boggling things to get his attention. However, he was believing that he would find his wife when the time was right. He never thought he would find her on the side of the road crying. But when he went over to help and looked down at her, way deep down on the inside of him he heard a still small voice say, "Here is your wife."

Kevin escorted Niki down the aisle. Mark escorted Jada. The groom and his father were standing at the alter waiting for the bride. The trumpets rang out "Here Comes the Bride." All eyes looked towards the back door. In came Erica, riding sidesaddle on a white horse. Gasping went on all over the congregation. Cameras flashed non-stop.

Niki's mouth dropped open. "You go, girl" she yelled. Fortunately, she couldn't be heard above the trumpets. *How the heck had Erica managed to keep this secret?*

Jada just smiled elegantly, nodding her head, saying to herself, "That's my girl."

When the horse arrived at the altar, Richard reached up and lifted his bride down ever so suavely. He was so debonair.

As the trainer led the horse out through a side door, the bridal party took their places. The service was beautiful.

As Richard bent over to salute his bride, there was a loud noise, then total darkness. Immediately, as light was restored, those that remained saw not a soul, just empty clothes, at the altar. They saw empty clothes in the seats.

Those who were left knew what had happened and began to cry out, "OH, GOD, NO! HELP US, PLEASE! JESUS, PLEASE, JESUS," they screamed.

In a number of cell blocks at the Women's Correctional Facility in Fulton, Virginia, there were empty clothes on the beds. In one of these cells, there was a heart drawn on the wall. Inside the heart was written…Rae Loves Jesus.

For the Lord himself shall descend from heaven with a shout, with the voice of the archangel, and with the trump of God: and the dead in Christ shall rise first: Then we which are alive and remain shall be caught up together with them in the clouds, to meet the Lord in the air: and so shall we ever be with the Lord. Wherefore, comfort one another with these words.

1 Thessalonians 4:16-18